HEROINES OF INDIA

HEROINES OF INDIA

MANMATHA NATH DUTT, Shastri, M. A.

GYAN

Published by

Gyan Publishing House
5, Ansari Road
Daryaganj, New Delhi-110002
Phone: 011-47034999, 9811692060
E-mail: books@gyanbooks.com

Distribution Network
gyanbooks.com
India, USA, Canada, UK, Australia, France

ISBN: 978-81-212-8686-2 (PB)
First Published, 1908

2nd Impression 2023

Printed at: Gyan Press, Delhi.

HEROINES OF INDIA
Author: Manmatha Nath Dutt, Shastri

HEROINES OF IND.

HEROINES OF IND.

THIRD EDITION.

BY

MANMATHA NATH DUTT, Shastri, M.A.,

RECTOR, KESHUB ACADEMY,

Author of the English Translations of the Ramayana, Mahabharata, Srimadbhagavatam, Vishnupuranam and other works.

CALCUTTA:

THE SOCIETY FOR THE RESUSCITATION OF INDIAN LITERATURE.

3, FURIAPUKUR STREET, P. O., SHAMBAZAR.

1908

To

Babu

Guru Prosunno Ghose,

Jorabagan, Calcutta.

My dear friend,

I know, you always take a sincere interest in all educational works of our country. Your sympathy with oriental publications is also equally well-known. I am really happy in dedicating this little volume to you as a token of my esteem for many genial qualities that I have seen in you.

Yours very sincerely,

1st Nov. 1893. } *Manmatha Nath Dutt,*

PREFACE.

We are very glad to say that our attempt to popularise Indian Classics has met with immense success. In the course of six months the first edition of our "TALES OF IND" has been all sold. We have received encouragement from all sides. We, therefore, hasten to place a few more volumes of the "Gleanings" before our readers. But we must mention that we have to make some changes in our original plan of action. We have removed *Sati* and *Srikrisna* from the "Tales" and placed them in their proper places in subsequent volumes. We have tried every means to make these volumes acceptable to our readers and we sincerely hope that our "Heroines" would meet the same kind reception as was kindly vouchsafed to its predecessor.

CALCUTTA,

1st Nov. 1893.

CONTENTS.

INTRODUCTORY SKETCHES.

PART I.

[1]

If you traverse India from one end to another, you will enjoy her beautiful scenery and magnificent ruins, but far more beautiful than all this,—than the wild romantic scenery of hills and dales, than the magnificent painting in stone, the world renowned Tajmahal, than the wonderful works of sculpture within the caves of Ellora, and the extensive ruins that lie scattered round the ancient cities of Delhi and Agra,—far more beautiful than all this are the beauties of the Hindu Home. There were gems and jewels in India which were the wonders of the human race, but far more beautiful and far more precious than all this is the Hindu

Wife. She is the purest of all the gems that were ever found in any part of the world.

The brief narratives of the characters and careers of some of those that have been reckoned as heroines in the pages of history,—those whose names have come down from generation to generation as the glorious productions of woman-hood and those whom the people of India adore, admire and cherish as the idols of their worship, would show that they were none but the Hindu wives. In the royal palaces of potentates and kings, in the poverty-stricken cottages of the poor,—everywhere and in every shade of Hindu society—heroines abound, —but a very few of them only have been delineated in the pages of history.

The life of a Hindu girl from her birth to death is a continuous string of religious trainings ;—she is taught bravery and courage, fidelity and obedience, benevolence and kindness, simplicity and innocence,—above all she is taught all that ennobles a human heart and raises it to the level of gods and angels. Every Hindu wife is a heroine,—nay she is an angel ; therefore we find in India noble heroines equal of whom we cannot find any where else. We are bound, before we proceed further and before we mention some particular instances, to paint a Hindu Wife,

—to delineate the class and to pay the tributes of admiration to the altar on which she stands.

Early morning: the sun is just peering from behind the cluster of trees guilding their green leaves with glittering gold and throwing his magnificient light on village homes. Every Indian house, be it a royal palace or a thatched hut, has a yard at the centre. At the centre of this yard sits a girl, her age being only seven. Her long black hair; flow down her back and play in ringlets over her shoulders and breast; they are all wet indicating that she has just bathed. She has painted her beautiful fore-head with sweet scented sandal, and a fancy colored silken cloth adorns her body. On her right, on a copper plate, there are flowers of sorts, which she herself has gathered from various trees; on her left on another there are rice, fruits and sweets. It is the Hindu New year's day, and she is worshipping the great God of *Kailash*, praying for his blessings and for a husband as good and great as He. When she recites her prayers in her sweet silvery voice, in her native simplicity and religious enthusiasm, clasping both of her hands, kneeling on her knees and raising her apealing eyes towards heaven, it is a picture worthy of a Raphael's pen. Thus she worships every day till the end of the month and every year till she is married.

[2]

The next great event in her life is her marriage. The sounds of music rise above the noise of the household; the elders are smoking with all the gravity of busy men and receiving the guests with all the grace of oriental courtesy. Boys and girls in their holy-day attire frisk about the door; they laugh, they chat, they run to see how far still is the bridegroom with his merry folks. There in the Zenana matrons bustle about, doing a thousand nameless things and maidens peep through the windows to catch the first glimpse of the happy bridegroom.

He comes in the garb of an ascetic; a red silken cloth is round his body, the garlands of white flowers are round his neck, his forehead is painted with the fragrant sandal. He comes to perform a solemn religious ceremony,—the gravest and the most serious event of his life.

He has passed the day in worshipping gods and godesses and the departed spirits of his dead forefathers. He had prayed for their blessings on him and on her, whom he is going to marry. And she too has kept the day in religious devotions, fasting and doing naught which is unholy and impure. There is nothing grosser, nothing material, nothing of the human passions that bind us to this material world. It is a ceremony which celebrates the happy union of two souls on their way to heaven, —souls which are born and destined for each other, not for this world alone, but for ever and for eternity.

Face to face they sit; the father has given away his dearly loved child to his son-in-law and he has accepted the precious gift. The reverend priest joins their hands and folds round them the garlands of flowers, chains too strong to be ever broken. Fire is ablaze, incense is burnt, gods and goddesses are invoked, and fire, water, wind, ether and all the elements are called to be witness. Then he prays to Him who rules over all this vast universe, both material and spiritual, to come and bless the holy nuptials. The bridegroom fully believing that he is in the presence of the great Spirit and standing before His majestic throne begins to recite the *mantras*, the solemn oath, which ends with "for eternity we shall be flesh to flesh and soul to soul." His voice trembles and the solemn word vibrates through his heart. He clasps the soft hand which is within his bound in flowery chains, for courage and strength, and she, though she hardly understands all that is said, instinctively knows that she is no longer what she was. Her childish hand trembles like an aspen leaf and her heart beats as if it would burst. She shuts her eyes in fear and awe and prays to that great God to whom she has been praying from her childhood.

[3]

She suddenly finds herself surrounded on all sides by strangers. Wherever she casts her weeping eyes she sees strange faces and strange scenes. She has come to her husband's home,—a thorough strange place, but a new world of bliss. Amidst all her mental agonies she longs for night, for in her childish heart she instinctively knows that with night will come the time when she will meet him who is no longer a stranger to her and with whom she will feel herself no longer alone. Her heart beats quicker and her blood runs faster, as night clad in her sable mantle, slowly steps in on the earth. Amidst all the merry-makings of the household and melodies of music, two hearts throb in expectation and fear.

It is not the meeting of two youthful lovers who long to clasp each other in ardent embraces and cover each with hot and passionate kisses. It is like the first meeting of Adam and Eve on the celestial garden of Eden. He knows not whom he is to meet, but he longs to meet her and love her. And she, innocent as a child, waits in a baited breath to place her childish head on the breast of him who will be her Lord for ever and for eternity, and whom to love and obey she is born and destined. There is no choice, there is no selection,—he for her and she for him is their *faith* grown and developed from their very birth. It is the meeting of two streamlets which run at a distance, but which suddenly meet on account of the peculiar nature of the soil and which thenceforth are to flow together till the end of days. In the magnificent and beautiful garden of Eden, Adam was not more eager to meet his affianced Eve, than the Hindu husband before his happy *Flower-bed.* Beautiful Eve's angelic heart beat not more quickly when Adam stood before her than that of the Hindu girl, who bedecked with flowers, when sees her husband on this memorable night.

But painful parting and woeful separation follows. She lives with her parents and never sees her husband. The newly married wife lives with her parents for a year before she goes to live with her husband. The germ of love that is implanted in the hearts of the married pair on the happy night of the *Flower-bed* silently and slowly developes on account of the separation, both hearts yearing to meet together and the yearing daily grews stronger.

At last the special day for entertaining sons-in-law,—the celebrated Hindu festival of *Jamai Shasti*—comes. The husband goes to meet his wife after a long separation. Face to face they stand, but there are no ardent embraces and not kisses; there are no endearing terms and lying flatteries. They clasp each others hands and lie down side by side like two innocent children, their joys beaming in their eyes, their love being too deep for outward manifestations. Their love is the calm and serene love of children and not the flaming and maddening love of youth. They talk and talk on,—perhaps of dogs, cats and birds, perhaps of books, tales and annals and perhaps of brothers, sisters and friends. They talk on till Moon in her rosy magnificience appears on the horizon and light peeps into their bed to tell them that they are to part. They kiss each other and part,—not to meet again for some months.

She at last comes to her husband's house, and thence forth her life is a life of continual love and caresses. The best loved person in a Hindu household is its newly married wife. She is the darling of all and she is the beauty of the house. Her father-in-law brings for her ornaments and cloths, her brothers-in-law give her fancy toys and funny dolls, her sisters-in-law try to amuse her and her mother-in-law neglects her house-wifery to make her happy. She is the joy of her husband and of all those that live in his house. Boys and girls, men and women all vie with one another to please her and make her happy. Wherever she goes it becomes a land of joy and whoever she meets becomes the happiest of beings.

It is night; she sits at his feet and he is engaged in his works. She silently sews and looks up now and then at his face with eyes full of delicious joy. She wishes that his work is done, but does not breathe, lest it disturbs him. How glad would she be to talk to him! But she has been taught to consider his works far more important than all her selfish wishes. She knows she is to help him in his worldly affairs and not to put obstacles in his way.

Night wears on,—sleep slowly steps into her eyes. She places her head on her husband's lap and roams into the magic land of dreams. He sits motionless, lest his movements disturb her calm repose. Lovely smiles play on her lips and joy beams out from her childish face. How happy is he to contemplate the lovely countenance of his loving wife, sleeping so happily upon his lap!

There are storms in the atmosphere and tempests in the sea; there are painful partings and woeful separations in the highest perfection of domestic life. She has sobbed and wept, she has shed hot and bitter tears, hiding her face within the bosom of her beloved husband. She wept for hours and for the whole night.

She sobs as if her heart would break. There is no more time to lose, for perhaps, he is to catch a train. He tenderly and softly extricates himself from her loving grasp and escapes from the painful scene. He dares not give her a parting look, for his heart is full. And she, like a rose torn from the tree, fades and withers away. She fades away for the want of the merry smiles of her husband; she keeps hidden within her bosom the bitter pangs of separation. None knows how much she suffers! Her grief knows no expression. The wound that bleeds in her heart can only be guessed from the melancholy shadow that swims over her ever-smiling countenance. She neglects her toilet and forgets her ornaments; she moves about the house as a shadow, the substance of which is carried away.

[5]

She is the servant of the house and the servant of all works. All the works of the house from the lowest to the highest are exclusively hers. Hardly then remains anything for any one else to do. She knows no rest,—she knows not what it is to neglect or shirk her duties. None tells her what to do; she knows her works and does them better than any one else. She does this and that, she is here, there and everywhere. Who knows how to make a house cheery and happy better than she? If there were no such obedient and willing servants in the Hindu homes, the Hindus would have been at a loss to know what to do!

She is the mistress of the house, and a most loving mistress she is! Her husband earns money, he toils day and night and there ends his labour. He is quite at his ease as soon as he places the money in her judicious hands. Such a willing servant and loving mistress can hardly be found. She commands, she works, in her domestic arrangements and in her household affairs, she is the sole mistress of her husband's purse. She can squander it, she can hoard it, she can use it in whatever way she likes. Who is so economical, who knows so well the proper use of money, who is so good in making a house comfortable if she is not the Hindu wife? She is the servant, she is the mistress,—nay she is the wealth of Hindu homes.

The Hindu wife stands in her home with her loving arms spreading around her,—under the peaceful shade of which come and gather fathers and sons, brothers and sisters, nephews and nieces and various other kith and kin. She is the connecting link of the chains of men and women that usually form a Hindu Joint Family. They are men of various habits and various tastes, each of whom receives from her all he wants and finds nothing to complain of. She is the ruling queen of every Hindu household and her will is law to all that live in and around her happy home.

She is the embodiment of all that is good and great in this world. Well, she is a heroine, not only in courage and bravery, not only in fidelity and charity, not only in benevolence and kindness, intelligence and capacity, she is a heroine in faith and love—love towards the Heavenly Father, and faith in her ever-loving husband.

And how beautiful, grand and sublime is she! The soft rays of the morning sun play on the wavy breast of the beautiful river that flows towards the sea through the fertile plains of Ind. The green leaves of innumerable trees on both the banks stoop down towards the water, as if to give her a parting kiss. Narrow winding paths from the neighbouring houses come through the silvan vistas to the very edge of the water. Along these paths the Hindu wife goes back home with her pitcher of water. The villagers move away from her path and respectfully stand by to let her pass. She moves on like a proud queen speaking to none and looking at none; she stops and draws down her veil and stands aside, only when she meets any of those whom she is to respect and revere. She goes and kneels at the door of the household god and prays for his blessings,—her prayers come out from the very depth of her heart. Then as if sure of receiving the blessings, she enters the house in lighter steps and joyous smiles.

Graceful female forms are often seen passing along the village paths and the village afternoons are always sweetened with the music of their ornaments. When her husband leaves her to take a walk or to meet a friend, she too goes out to pay visits to her neighbours,—here to an ill relative and there perhaps to a poor woman. She is the ministering angel not to her husband alone, but to all that live around her happy home.

In the unknowable mystery of destiny she often becomes a widow, and widowhood is but another shade of the Hindu marriage. Her belief is that marriage is not for this world alone, but for eternity and her husband is her husband for ever-lasting time, through innumerble births and deaths.

No ornament adorns her arms, a piece of white cloth is round her body, a flower basket hangs in her left hand and the right is busy in gathering the best gifts of Nature which are the most favourite offerings for gods and goddesses. She hastens towards the river,—she bathes, she prays, she worships and bows down her head to the rising Sun. She goes back home, her long black hairs flow down her back and breast; her face beams with celestial fire. She is the help-mate of all her neighbours; she gladly joins in their works and helps them with all her might. She is always to be found in the house where cooking is necessary for a general feast. Who knows how to cook better than she!

She silently moves about amongst the neighbouring houses of the poor. She helps some in their works ;—she talks with some and tells them all about God and Religion. To one she gives some rice, to another some vegetables,—thus she passes the day in her own good charities. If one in the house or in the neighbourhood is ill, she hastens to his side with all her motherly smiles. She takes care of him, she nurses him, she gives him medicine ; she never leaves his side till he is all right. Who knows nursing so well as she? Who knows how to smooth the path of a dying man Who is she if she is not the Hindu widow !

She is the mother of all the children of the neighbourhood and her love flows like an autumnal river that overflows its banks and innundates the country. In the evening when all the world is returning to rest, she recites melodious incantations, sweet prayers and sublime odes of adoration. Boys and girls come round her to hear her religious tales.

She is an ascetic, she takes her meal only once a day,—it consists of neither fish nor flesh, it is the simplest of simple fares. Her life is a life full of spirituality and her thoughts are full of purity and philanthropy. She is the presiding goddess and the ruling angel of the Hindu home.

Thus each and every one of the Hindu wives

can safely be called a great and good heroine,—a heroine not only in name but in every angelic quality. And why should they not be heroine, why should not some excel all others and earn everlasting fame in the pages of history, when they have such a grand and great model placed before them as their favourite goddess *Sati?* And who is she? Before we narrate the life and career of those who have been imortalised in the pages of history by their noble deeds, heroic conducts and angelic love, faith, fidelity and benevolence we must see her who moulds the character of the Hindu wives.

PART II.

We cannot write the history of the Indian heroines, unless we narrate the deeds and tell the history of the Heroine of all the heroines, the greatest of all the great women of the world,—we mean the Goddess, whose figure adorns most of the temples of India. She is worshipped as the Mother of the universe, as *Sakti*,—the invisible and unknowable Force of Creation,—as the unconcievable great ONE who is the Soul of all souls. She is worshipped by the mildest of the mild and the gentlest of the gentle as the Goddess of mercy and kindness; she is worshipped by the wickedest of the wicked as the Goddess of fury and carnage. She is the only One whom both the good and the bad equally adore.

This Goddess of all goddesses, this *Sati*,—who has innumerable other names,—is the Heroine of India! Others that followed her, either in the path of giving protection to the weak or destroying the wicked, either to love their husbands or to make their home happy, either for patriotism, bravery or strength of character, followed her noble footsteps. It is She who moulds the character of all Hindu women and who rules over all Hindu homes.

North of the *Himâlayas,* in the land of beauty and sublimity, there was a charming hill, called the *Kailâsh.* It was the land of angels and fairies; it was the land of many colored flowers and folliage; it was a lovely bower of Nature's own making, where she had congregated all that was beautiful and all that was lovely and charming in the animal or in the botanic kingdom.

In this land of love, beauty and pleasure *Siva* and his beloved wife *Sati* had their happy home. It was but a cottage on the top of a snowy range; it was a hut, covered with twining creepers. There was not the least artificial effort to secure any of the worldly comforts. But Nature was the obedient maid in this poor but the happiest home. She had gathered for their frugal meals all the sweet fruits of the world round their hut; she had come with all her flowers to decorate their nuptial bed; she had placed in their lovely bower all the singing birds of the sky to pour into their ears the sweetest music of the world.

But *Siva* had given up all that was worldly. Well, he was the richest man of the world;

he was the wisest of all the wise and the mightiest of all the mighty; he had no wants to complain of. But he had left all this far behind him and had made his abode in the solitude of *Kailásh*, away from all worldly wealth and cares.

He wore a piece of tiger's skin; he sat on that of a lovely deer; round his neck hung the garlands of bones; he was entwined with deadly snakes and serpents. He rode an old bull and begged from door to door; he looked like a maniac. To him all the horrors of the world were welcome.

But he was a mighty man; he ruled over the Matter and controlled the Spirit. He was the perfect developement of Intellect;—always deeply engaged in his own thoughts, he cared nought for the world around. He had forgotten that there existed a universe; he was intoxicated with the wine of his own thoughts—and that thought consisted of meditating upon his own dear wife *Sati*. He had forgotten that he or any other being did exist; he felt that only ONE existed and that ONE was his lovely wife *Sati*.

He had two faithful attendants, named *Nandi* and *Bhringi*; he was sorrounded with innumerble ghosts and spirits; he was feared and respected all over the world. But look to the side of this horrible and fearful figure; there will you find seated smiling and happy a goddess, quite the reverse of this terrible one.

It was *Sati*, the daughter of king *Daksha*, one of the mightiest rulers of the earth. There is no language which can adequately describe her most wonderful beauty. But no jewellery adorned her hair; no ornaments her body. Her black long hair flowed in beautiful ringlets down her back and breast;—round her neck there were some garlands of beads and round her loins and body was a piece of rag.

She had given up all her paternal royal luxuries,—she had become a poor beggar and a great ascetic like her husband dear. She lived with him happy and her home in *Kailâsh* was the happiest in the world.

They had risen above the broils of the world; they had gone beyond the all-grasping hand of Mysery. They soared high in a place where nothing worldly, material or gross could reach them. They were the happiest beings and their home breathed in perfect bliss.

They had no wants, for they had destroyed all wants; they lived in the world, but had wiped away the idea of its existence from their minds. They had achieved that grand knowledge which told them that this perceptible universe was only a mental dream of the Supreme Being, having had no real existence of its own. They felt the grand truth which told them that they were not separate beings; they were that GREAT ONE who only is real and who only does exist.

All worldly matters had fled from their lovely home; nothing savouring of the material world could dare approach their grand *Kailásh*. They lived very happy in the Land of intellect and in the happy valley of salvation and bliss.

Thus lived *Siva* and *Sati* for many years on the snowy heights of their happy *Kailâsh*, till an unhappy incident occurred. Once on a time *Siva* happened to attend a great *Yagma* where his father-in-law, king *Daksha*, was present. He was a man having his mind not in the world around. He did not observe the approach of his father-in-law and forgot to show him the proper respect. The proud king took offence; he was never pleased with his mad son-in-law. Learning that the horrible man, whom he took to be a great *Yogee* and to whom he gave his most beloved daughter in marriage, had made his *Sati* worse than a beggar, he gave up all communications with him. He studiously used to avoid him and told people that his daughter was dead. But when he saw his mad son-in-law openly insulting him by not according to him the ordinary courtesy of the society, he resolved to teach him a lesson.

He held a *Yagma*, in which he invited all the world except *Siva*, and his wife poor *Sati*. There were great preparations and grand amusements; it was one of the greatest festivities ever held in this world; it was a festivity in which all the people of the world were specially invited to join, except the mad man of the *Kailâsh*. All the relatives and friends of the great king came; all the princesses of the royal household arrived from their husbands' homes, except poor *Sati*, who was not even informed of the great festivities that her beloved father was holding.

But *Nârada* went to *Kailâsh* and informed her what was going on at her father's palace. *Sati* grew eager to go,—she had not seen her mother and sisters for many years past; she felt that her absence in this great festivity would be deeply felt by her dear mother, if not by any one else.

She went to her husband and told him all that she had heard from *Nârada*. She entreated him to allow her to go and see her parents. "My poor darling," said *Siva*, "Your father has purposely forgotten to invite us. He wants to heap insults upon *Siva*, to whom insults are honours. But *Sati*, why should you go and be insulted before all your relatives and friends ?" "My dear husband," replied she, "Should a daughter mind, whether her father invites her or not? Is there any necessity for a daughter to seek for an invitation when she goes to see her parents?"

Siva smiled and said, "I shall not prevent you from going to your parents. But *Sati*, remember that you are going to a great trial. Be very careful and try to come back as soon as possible." Then he turned to *Nandi* and ordered him to go with her. "*Nandi*," said he, "Take care to control your temper. There will you find all that wealth and worldly vanity can produce. You and *Sati* will appear in that grandeur and pomp like two of the poorest beggars of the world. People may naturally redicule you,—nay they may slight you or perhaps insult you. Do not mind all this? Come back with *Sati* as soon as possible." They left *Kailâsh,—Sati* on the back of the old Bull, *Nandi* leading him to the palace of king *Daksha*.

Beyond and above the world this asceticism is very grand; but in a place where the wealth and riches of the world had come to vie with one another, where the great chiefs and potentates had come together with all their showy costumes and invaluable jewelleries, *Sati's* appearance looked like something very hateful. Especially to king *Daksha*, it was really painful,—nay insulting to find his own daughter present in that grand assembly in a plight worse than that of a beggar.

They entered the great palace, now alive with men and women. They passed through the crowd in silence,—alas, none welcoming them! Their slight and neglect were apparent on all sides; many whispered amongst themselves and many began to abuse *Siva,* who had made a royal princess a beggar.

She went to her mother, who came running to welcome her,—she being the most beloved of all her children. But she was horrified to see the beggarly state of her daughter; she stood a few seconds wildly staring at her and then she fainted. Then arose wild weepings all over the palace; *Sati* had come unasked and uninvited, but she had come as a beggar!

[2]

Queen *Prasuti* asked her daughter to give up her beggarly costume. She brought for her beautiful jewelleries and gold-embroidred clothes; she brought for her various delicacies, those that were her favourites when she was a child. But *Sati* declined all. "Dear mother," said she, "I must first see my father and ask him why he has not invited us?"

She heard no refusal; she went to the grand assembly where king *Daksha* was engaged in the great *Yagma*.

Oh, what a contrast! Asceticism and worldliness stood side by side. The worldly pomp and grandeur stood face to face with solitude and calmness of retirement. Poverty was placed by the side of wealth.

Sati appeared in that grand assembly and all rose in respect. But king *Daksha* lost his temper. "Oh, shame, to me!" cried he, "Why did I not die before seeing my own daughter reduced to such an ignoble state! Who asked you to come here,—Oh you wicked girl, to me you are dead!" Then he turned towards the assembly and roared, "Look at the doings of the ruffian who calls himself a *Yogee.* Mad, wicked scoundrel,—always beastly intoxicated and piteously dirty, look, gentlemen, how he has reduced a Princess of the royal house of great *Daksha* to the lowest stratum of poverty!" "Father, dear father," appealed *Sati*, "Abuse me if you like, but do not abuse my husband. You yourself taught me in my early days that to a wife her husband, however bad he might be, is her God and Preceptor."

But king *Daksha* fired on; he did not care for the feelings of his poor daughter. She again and again tried to stop him, but finally seeing that it was inpossible to stop her enraged fafher from showering abuses over his dear husband's head,—she determined to give up her life. She preferred death to hearing such abuses of one who was her husband.

She stood in that great assembly as only a goddess could stand; she mentally meditated upon her husband and bade him farewell; she then turned towards the assembly and fell dead.

There were loud lamentations all over the palace;—people ran to see *Sàti* from all directions, Queen *Prasuti* came weeping with all her daughters. The joy and merriments were soon turned into sorrow and grief.

In the meanwhile *Nandi* hastened to *Kailásh*. *Siva* heard in silence of the death of his most beloved wife. He rose and rushed towards the kingdom of king *Daksha*, followed by all his ghosts and spirits.

Soon the mad hordes appeared before the assembly; in a minute the *Yagma* was destroyed, and the assembled guests were mercilessly beaten. King *Daksha* was attacked;—he was soon beheaded and the head of a goat was placed upon his shoulder. *Siva* took up the corpse of his dear wife, placed it on his shoulder and began to dance like a maniac.

He left the palace of king *Daksha* with the dead body and roamed over the world for many long years till it gradually fell piece by piece from his shoulder.

He then silently retired to his mountain home ;— and there sat he in his great *Yoga*. He entered into that grand sleep of eternal peace which lasted for hundreds of years.

[4]

There was overlasting feud between the gods and the demons; sometimes the gods were victorious and sometimes the demons,—but finally the demons grew invinsible under their great leader *Taraka*. Under him they marched to the gate of heaven and besieged the celestial regions.

The gods and the demons met, after a long period, like two wild whirlpools in a great storm. The war continued for years, both parties fighting, as only the gods and the demons could fight. Again and again the thunder was let loose, but to no purpose; the demons gradually gained ground. The celestial army was daily broken down and the gods were at last defeated and routed. They fled in hot haste towards heaven, pursued by the successful and elated demons.

They fled precipitously into their kingdom and shut up its gates; but alas, fortune was against them! The demons stormed their heavenly citadel, drove them out of their celestial homes, and took possession of the much-desired kingdom. The gods fled in all directions and were scattered over the universe. At last heaven was lost.

Indra, king of the gods, having been defeated and driven out of his kingdom, went to the Creator for advice and help. "My son," said he, "Do not be disheartened; such is the Will of Providence. *Siva* is immersed in great *Yoga* on the death of his wife; and this is the reason of the demons becoming unconquerable. Go to *Vishnu* and he will advise you as to what to do in order to regain thy Paradise."

Indra went to*Baikuntha* and prayed to its Lord for help. He narrated all that had happened and told him the miserable plight into which the gods and the goddesses had fallen. "My beloved son," said the great God, "I have no power to destroy; I can preserve and I have preserved you from death by bestowing upon you immortality. None can destroy the demons except *Siva.* His wife is born as a daughter of king *Himâlaya.* Go and try to get her married with the Great Destryor. The son that would be born of the marriage, would regain heaven for you."

The king of the gods returned to his hidden-place. There held he a confidential council with his ministers and generals; it was settled to despatch *Nárada* to king *Himàlaya* with the proposal of the marriage.

The blue water of the beautiful lake *Manasa Sarabàra* rolled on towards the grassy beach. The silvery waves danced in merriment and ran one after the other till they reached and kissed the leaves of bending boughs of flowery plants. Red, white, green and blue and lotuses smiled in their own sublime beauty; the wavy-necked swans glided over the water; some dived below, some got up and the waters fell from their milk-white plumes. Busy bees in their sweet music flew from one flower to the other; many coloured and many shaped birds had filled the place with their melodious cheerings. In the distance the hoary headed peaks of the majestic *Himàlayas* had risen one over the other. The rays of the setting sun played-over the snow-clad mountains. Nature in all her beauty had appeared in the land of snow and cold.

Beautiful *Uma*, the daughter of the Mountains,

had come to the lake with her playmates and companions to pray to the great God of all gods; she had come to adore and worship him and to join with Nature to sing his praise. When they were thus engaged in prayer, the great *Rishi Nàrada* appeared before them and bowed down his hoary head at the feet of the beautiful girl. She was offended,—it is an outrage to her feelings to see an old hoary headed *Rishi* salute her thus. But the *Rishi* hastened to apologise. "Mother," said he, "you are not only my mother, but the mother of all the universe. You know it,—why then frown at me so angrily!" *Uma* smiled and fled to her home.

The *Rishi* met the mountain-king and queen. He told them his message; he told them all that had happened in heaven; he told them, his *Uma* was no other than *Sati*, the great goddess of *Kailàsh*, born again to be joined with her husband. We need not say the king and the queen were too glad to give their consent to the happy nuptials. Old *Nàrada* returned to heaven with joy beaming from his face.

But the difficulty was not there;—the gods knew not what to do to rouse up *Siva* from his *Yoga*-sleep. "Oh, king," suggested one, "Take *Madan* with you. There is none in the universe who can withstand the arrows of Love. Surely *Siva's Yoga* would be broken and *Nârada* would be able to propose to him the marriage.

The suggestion was adopted and every arrangement was made. The chief gods went towards *Kailâsha* and *Nârada* promised to join them there.

On the heights of the hoary *Kailâsha* sat *Siva* in his great *Yoga*-sleep. Calmness reigned all over the place,—the sway of solitude having extended far and wide. Not a sound, not the least noise, could venture to disturb the peace of the awful place; the wind had ceased to breathe where the great Dostroyer sat in his majesty.

The gods silently and slowly assembled at the foot of the snowy heights. *Madan* was put forward. He advanced trembling from head to foot. But he gathered courage, took up his bow and sent up an arrow. It did its action: the Great Unknown was moved; he slowly opened his eyes and looked around. He saw the god of Love, slinking away from his sight. Uncontrolable anger rose up in his bosom, and his forhead emitted forth destructive fire. Soon the poor god of Love was overwhelmed with its deadly flames. Oh, how piteously he cried for help! how he appealed to the gods to save him from *Siva's* anger! But all was in vain!

But the *Yoga*-sleep of the great God was destroyed. He rose from his seat and moved towards his home. At this opportune moment, when the wound made by Love was fresh in his heart, *Nárada* greeted him and proposed the marriage. He told the great God how badly the universe was faring by his inactivity and his *Yoga*; how it had become urgently necessary for him to marry and settle down; how his wife had again taken birth as a daughter of king *Himálaya.*

Siva gave his consent and *Nárada* hastened to the gods to impart to them the welcome news. There was great joy amongst the gods and the goddesses; they all hastened from all quarters to be present at the wedding. It was solemnized in due form, the Creator himself acting as the high priest.

A son was born of this marriage and he was named *Kartikeya.* When he grew up, he was elected as the general of the heavenly hosts. Under him the gods received back their old courage and energy; and under his flag they rallied round, and hoped to regain their lost heaven.

Kartikeya led the gods to the gates of heaven and challenged the demons to battle. Another great war broke out and lasted for years, till at last the great *Tàraka* was killed and the demons were hopelessly defeated. They were driven out of the celestial kingdom and heaven was regained.

[4]

TIME went on and there was no disturbance in heaven. But the struggle of elements could never cease; the deadly feud between the gods and the demons could never end in peace and amity. A decade passed when two very powerful demons were born, who gathered round them all the demon chiefs and began to disturb the peace of heaven. King *Sambhu* and his brother *Nisambhu* gradually grew very powerful and extended their sway far and wide over the universe. They attacked once the gods, defeated and routed them in battle and made their position most uncomfortable and untenable in heaven. They were far more powerful than *Táraka*; infact the great Destroyer had honoured them by bestowing his great Spirit upon them which made them, on the one hand thoroughly invincible and irresistible; and on the other the very incarnation of destruction and evil. They possessed a General as great as themselves; the *Danava Raktabijá*, having secured from *Siva* the boon of having a *Raktabija* at each drop of his blood. Thus he was more than an immortal. The gods are not killed, but the General of king *Sambhu*, if wounded would produce a host of *Raktabijas*, as powerful as the orignal one. The gods lost heart and gradually began to fly from heaven. *Indra* hastened to *Brahmâ*, but he said that he really did not know what to advise. He hastened to *Vishnu* and asked permission to resign his throne and sceptre of heaven, if He did not protect him and the gods from the the oppressions of *Sambhu* and *Nishambhu*. "*Indra*," said the Preserver, "Twice have I pointed to you the way to defeat the *Danavas*. But really I do not know what to say now. As far as I see, *Sambhu* and *Nisambhu* cannot be killed, unless the great Destroyer does it himself. None can help you at this crisis except the Lord or the Lady of *Kailash*."

Who could dare go to the God of Destruction? *Indra* appeared before *Durgà*, the Lady of *Kailàsh*. She was moved by the piteous appeals of the gods and the goddesses. Finding no other way to check the oppressing and destroying power of the demon kings she agreed to go and fight with them. "My children," said she, "Go back to your heaven; remain at ease; for the good of the world I shall go and kill these two demon kings."

She appeared as a most beautiful damsel in the pleasure-garden of the demon king. Her exceptional beauty was more than what could be described; her voluptuous grace and her youthful loveliness filled the place with a sort of majesty and grandeur.

The report of her arrival soon reached the demon king. Great *Sambhu* grew mad to possess her; he immediately sent messengers to her, offering her his throne and kingdom. But she was not what they took her to be.

"Oh, beautiful lady," said the messenger, "Who art thou that hast graced our royal gardens?" The great goddess smiled and replied, "I am his who admires and adores me." "Then, Oh Lady," said the messenger, "Come to our king. I have been sent by him. He asks you to be his queen." "Go and tell him," said she, "I am only to be had by force. Whoever defeats me in battle, possesses me in peace."

When her bold words were reported to the king he smiled and took it for a joke. But in order to humour her, he ordered one of his great generals to go to her and escort her to the royal palace. But she challenged him to battle; the poor general was forced to fight and was killed.

King *Sambhu* was really astonished to learn that his general had been killed by a woman. He was not to be trifled with; he immediately ordered another of his generals to go with his army and bring the damsel to the royal court. But there was a great battle, and the general perished with all his army.

The king was really alarmed; he sent for his Commander-in-Chief, *Raktabija* and asked him to see what the matter was. The great *Dànava* went out with all his soldiers and found the Goddess quietly sitting, after destroying the demon army. He tried to induce her to come with him without further ado; but she declined and challenged him to battle. "Shame on me," said *Raktabija*, "If I fight with a woman.!" "But" replied she, "Try the game. I am more than a woman."

At last *Raktabija* was forced to fight and a terrible battle raged from morning to night. The Great Goddess fought as the great Spirit of Destruction could possibly fight. But, alas, all her efforts were fruitless, for she could not kill *Raktabija*;—in her efforts to kill him, she created innumerable *Raktabijas* to fight with her.

She at last appeared in her great *Kali*-form. She divided herself into innumerable *Kalis*; and all those *Kalis* began to fight in the greatest fury, some killing the demons and some drinking up their blood. Thus no more blood was dropped and no more *Raktabija* was created. By the evening the whole demon army with their great General had perished; and the Goddess, having withdrawn her forces, had turned again herself into a beautiful damsel.

We need not say, the demon king was much alarmed and much grieved by the sad fate of his great General. He gathered round him the rest of his great army and sallied forth to fight with the fell woman, who had suddenly appeared in his kingdom. We need not try to describe this battle, —a battle the equal of which had never occurred and which the greatest poets had failed adequately to describe. Suffice it to say that when the great *Sambhu* saw his beloved brother fall, he became ten times more furious. From morning to evening there was awful carnage and still there was not the least chance of success on the side of the goddess. Success be apart,—the demon king suddenly caught hold of the flowing black hair of the Great Goddess in the heat of the action; he raised her up and whirled her round by the head. She was defeated, she was mercilessly whirled and she hardly had time to breathe or to cry for help. Then she silently prayed for protection and help of his great husband *Siva*, who soon came to her rescuc. He immediately withdrew from the demon king the Spirit with which be blessed him. The great demon suddenly found him as weak as a child and was soon killed.

There was great joy amongst the gods and they lived happily in heaven.

But she had gone mad,—she was furious as fury itself; she was terrible as terror. She had destroyed the demon king and his wicked army, she had destroyed his kingdom and exterminated all that belonged to that terrible race. But she was not satisfied. The spirit of destruction had possessed her; she began to destroy the universe.

Then *Siva* came to stop her mad carreer. He lay down in the way by which she was rushing onward. She did not see him; she did see nothing. She rushed forward in her mad fury and placed her foot on the breast of her own dear husband. She looked down,—she felt the direst shame for her act,—she stopped and did not know what to do. *Siva* smiled and asked her to go with him to their *Kailash* which was dark and sad in her absence. She reasumed her beautiful and majestic shape and went with her beloved husband to their happy home.

But she was not a heroine of destruction only; —she was the protecting angel of all the weak and the good. She went to exterminate the demons, in order to protect the gods. When in the great monkey war after 10 years' struggle *Rama* could not rescue his wife from the clutches of the *Rakshasa* king, he worshipped the goddess on the shore of the blue ocean and prayed to her to come and protect him and his wife from the oppression of the wicked *Rakshasa*. The ever merciful, the ever protecting, the ever glorious Goddess at once came to his help. And thenceforth the arms of *Rama* became invincible; thenceforth victory smiled upon him and the wicked *Ravana* was killed with all his vicious race.

The happy home on the snowy *Kailasha* was soon echoed with the merry loughs of children. Two sons and two daughters had been born,—*Ganesh* was the great god of *all good*, *Kartekaya* was the generalissimo of the heavenly forces; beautiful *Lashkmi* was the goddess of wealth and accomplished *Sharashwati* was the goddess of learning. It is impossible for us to describe the domestic felicity and celestial bliss that pervaded through this family! Poets after poets and sages after sages have tried to paint the glory and happiness of *Kailash* and were all of opinion that they could not make the nearest approach to a true and real description of the happy family. The Hindu *Sastras* are full of graphic descriptions of the career and character of *Sati*,—they are read by thousands and sung in every village home. The Hindu breathes in the spirit of the *Kailash* and the Hindu wife lives in *Sati*.

Thus we find she is a goddess of mercy, of benovolence, of kindness,—nay of every good quality on which humanity stands. She is the best model to follow for the humanity; she is the grandest example of woman-hood; she is the greatest and the best heroine that the world has ever produced—nay she is *the* Goddess who is the source, who is the protectress, who is the final rest of this visible universe.

THE HEROINES OF IND.

A GROUP FROM THE PAST.

[1]

LET us go back the over-flowing stream of Time and see some of the great heroines that were born to cast a halo around humanity. They were women that attained the highest glory of womanhood ; they were angels that had left foot-prints on the sands of time. Time has done its works ; we know them only by name. Their works, all but destroyed, live amongst us in fragments and in parts, as so many ruins of a magnificent structure.

Four thousand years ago, when humanity was in its childhood,—when Europe, Asia, America and Africa were in darkness of ignorance,—when men lived like wild animals in the recesses of forests, preying on birds and beasts,—when there was no education, no civilisation, no religion on the face of the earth,—a race of men lived on the banks of the five rivers, the modern Province of the Punjab. They rose above all other races of mankind in education and civilisation. When people were too ignorant to know what this world really is, when they wondered in wild astonishment to see the magnificent panorama of Nature and fell into a sate of great terror on seeing her wild fury, the ever-merciful Providence declared himself through the lips of these men and women, who lived in the land of the five rivers.

They were far above the other races, and composed and sang some verses,—full of the Spirit of God, His mercy and His unknowable power. They sang,—"Whom should we worship and adore but Him, whose prowess the snow-clad mountains declare and whose glory the blue ocean and beautiful rivers sing!

Again,—

"He, is *One*, although He bears the name of many Gods. There is only *One*, who lived and breathed without the help of air, supported by Himself."

These songs, that are known by the name of *Vedas*, are the father of all religions. They are the first light that dawned on the earth; they are the first Spirit of God that fell on mankind. Some of these glorious songs were composed by women.— Can we not call them the angels of humanity ?

One of them is *Bishyabará* ; she was the author of the second song of the 5th chapter of the Rig Veda, which contains twenty-eight most beautiful stanzas.

Another is *Bak* ; she was the daughter of Rishi *Ambhrina* and the auther of 125th song in the 10th Chapter of the Rig Veda. The stanzas contain the highest ideal of the conception of God. The great commentators of these songs have said that they are the root of the *Vedanta* Philosophy. She lived a life of an ascetic and passed her days in prayers and meditations.

Another is *Lopa Mudra* ; she was the author of 79th song of the Rig Veda, containing two most excellent stanzas. She was the daughter of the king of *Kidarva* and the wife of great *Rishi Kgastya.* Though she was a princess, born and bred in luxury, she lived with her husband as an ascetic and followed him as a shadow.

There are many more whom we need not mention ; but these were the women that left behind them glorious examples of womanhood in all its phases,—as mother, as daughter, as sister, as wife, and as the presiding angel of a happy home. Their lives have been recited by the sages of old,—their examples have been followed by women of latter days; their words still vibrate through the literature of every race.

[2]

The people that lived on the banks of the five rivers gradually rose to a very high standard of civilisation. Grand and magnificent systems of Philosophy were found; benificent laws were laid down and a religion was preached, which was grandest in perception and sublimest in conception.

As in the days of yore, they were still proud of their women. *Maitri,* the wife of the great sage, *Jagmabalka,* was a woman of extraordinary intellect and erudition. *Jagmabalka* had another wife, named *Katyani,*—but she used to look after the house and was loved by *Maitri* as her own sister.

When the sage expressed his wish to retire and pass his life in a jungle, his wives were asked to devide amongst them all his properties. "My lord," said *Maitri*, "Can all the riches of the world give immortality?" "No, *Maitri*," said the Rishi, "that they cannot." "Then my Lord," replied she, "What would we do with the wealth that you want to give us?" Then she went on discussing with her husband many crude points of Mental Philosophy and the unknowable things of the Universe. Her discourse with her husband is still read with wonder by the great scholars all over the civilised world.

But there was a greater woman than *Maitri*. When *Jagmabalka* rose above all other sages, on account of his deep learning and unequalled devotion, he had to bow down his head before a woman. Her name was *Gargi*. What could be more lamentabe than the fact that we know nothing of her, except that she was the daughter of *Rishi Bachukun*. She was the author of a philosophical treatise and the great antagonist of *Jagmabalka* in the court of king *Janaka*.

Janaka was the king of *Mithila*; he was not only powerful in arms and statesmanship, but he was a great scholar in Philosophy and Theology. Even great *Rishis* used to repair to his court to learn from him many things which the Bramhin sages did not know. Once at a time he solemnised a great *Jagma* and invited all the sages from all parts of the country to honour the ceremony by their gracious presence. He brought one thousand cows with ten gold *mohars* attached to the horns of each, and placed them at the gate of the *Jagma* hall. He then said that he, who was the greatest believer in God, was at perfect liberty to take them away. None rose;—all sat silent, till *Jagma*-

balka asked one of his pupils to remove the cows. All other Brahmins took offence and were much displeased to see the insolence of *Jagmabalka,*—but none dared question his conduct. At last a woman rose from the corner of the assembly, and all eyes were directed to her. She was *Gargi.* "*Jagmabalka,*" said she, "Are you the greatest believer in God amongst us all?" Then she went on questioning him and there was a grand discussion between the two. We still possess this great debate,—but nothing else of the great *Gargi.*

[3]

Debahuti was the daughter of *Manu,* the great Hindu Law-Maker. *Manu* was a very powerful king, but his most favourite daughter *Debahuti* selected for her husband a poor *Rishi* of the forest. His name was *Kardama*; he was a man well-versed in learning and unmatched in asceticism and devotion. But for the sake of the Princess and for her great love towards him, he agreed to marry her, and the ceremony was solemnised in due form. She left her father's palace and went away with her husband to his cottage, which was situated in the deep forest.

Perhaps she married him for his great learning, for from her childhood she was fond of study.

When she grew up, her thirst for learning increased and she resolved to try the path of asceticism and to penetrate into the great Mystery of the Universe. Had she remained a Princess, she might have the advantages of tution from all the great sages of the age, but she would have very little chance of knowing Him, to which she aspired. Here in the forest with her husband, she got the best opportunity. She assiduously engaged herself in studying all that was worth studying, and practising all that gave her an idea of the great Source of this Universe.

We need not say how great she became. She gave birth to a son, who was virtually the father of all Philosophies,—for before him Philosophy was unknown to mankind. The name of his son is *Kapila,* the auther of the celebrated *Sankhya* Philosophy,—a Philosophy which for the first time in this world tried to analyse the human mind, to find out the causes of its pleasure and pain, and to point out the means of removing misery and of securing eternal bliss. *Debahuti* made *Kapila* what *Kapila* was; she taught him, when he was a child, things that opened before him a magnificent vista, through which he saw the salvation of humanity. When *Kapila* grew up, he plodded through the path pointed out by his great mother and at last found out the means of making mankind happy. It was about three thousand years ago that *Debahuti*, as an angel from heaven, placed, through her son on the plains of India, a foundation on which a magnificent structure was afterwards raised.

A few hundred years after, another great woman gave birth to a son as great and good as *Kapila* was. Her name was *Bishista;* she was the mother of the great Hindu Preacher and Reformer, *Sankarâcherya.* In the year of Christ 788 at *Chitamber* in the Deccan, *Sankar* was born. He lost his father in his childhood and was indebted to his mother for all that he learnt and did. Hardly had he attained sixteenth year when he became a great scholar and wrote commentaries on many great works. His great learning and erudition were unequalled by any man, before or after him. He brought the *Vedanta* Philosophy to the greatest prominence, and it was he who gave life to the dying Hinduism. When he was born, India was converted into Budhism;—Hunduism was no where to be found,—the Hundu Theology was no better than dead. But it was *Sankar* who gave fire to the Hindu Theology and life to the Hindu Religion. He cleared Buddhism off the face of India. And from the snow-clad Himalayas to the dark blue ocean, his preachings rose above all the dins of contending factions.

At his sixteenth year *Sankar* became an ascetic and went forth on his grand mission. After sixteen years he returned to his dying mother and told her what he had been able to do. What else could make the dying moments of a mother pleasant! She made *Sankar* what he was; and what was more pleasant to her than his success!

[4]

We shall now mention another who is respected all over the world. Her name was *Lilâbati*; she was the daughter of the great mathematician of ancient India, *Bhaskarâchârya.* He wrote a book on mathematics and named it after his beloved daughter. It is supposed that *Bhaskara* was born in 1115 A. D.

Lilâbati was a widow. Her great father knew through the vast knowledge that he possessed of astrology that if his daughter was married at a certain time she was sure to lose her husband. He determined not to give her away at that fatal moment. To know the exact time he placed a *Thambi** on a pot of water. It would be filled with water through a very fine bore which was at the bottom of it, but as destiny would have it, the great man's

* It was an instrument that served the purpose of a clock.

attempt to avert it became futile. When *Lilâbati* looked at it to see how the water was coming up, a small pearl fell into it from an ornament in her hair. It stopped the bore and none noticed it. When the time came to examine the *Thambi*, it was not filled; it was then examined and the pearl was detected. *Lilâbati* was, however, married and soon after she became a widow.

She then devoted herself to the study of mathematics under her father. Her father's great book, *Lilâbati*, which was addressed to her, shows what great mastery she got over the difficult science. It is said that she could tell the number of leaves of a tree by mathematical calculation. She passed her life in study, and mathematics was the God of her worship and adoration.

We shall mention another; her name was *Bhânumati*. As *Lilabati* was great in mathematics,—so *Bhanumati* was great in magic. She was the wife of Bhoj Raja,—a chieftain who ruled in Behar. It is a pity that we do not know much of her, except some anecdotes on which no reliance could be placed. *Bhoj Raja* flourished about two thousand years ago;—*Bhânumati* popularised magic at a time when all the world was in darkness; but still in every village and in every town where a magician is to be found, her memory is adored and worshipped with reverence and awe. No Indian magician would begin his show without a prayer for her blessings.

[5]

The name of *Khaná* is known as the greatest of all astrologers, though she was but a woman. She rose over all other astrologers of her age. Her verses are very popular and well-known to all.

But who is this *Khaná?* No body knows who were her parents. It is said that she was brought up by the Non-Aryan people, the *Rakshasas* and was taught astrology, in which they were great adepts. In fact at the early period of Aryan civilisation the *Rishis* were far behind in astrology than the Non-Aryan people whom they hated.

Khaná was an extraordnary genius ; her memory was unmatched and her intelligence was ever to be envied. She did not while away her time in playing; she assiduously studied astrology from her foster-father and soon became an adept in it.

There was another Aryan boy amongst the Non-Aryans and he lived in the same village in which *Khaná* lived. He was called *Mihir*, and was a great favourite of all the *Rakshasas*. He too learnt astrology and became a great astrologer.

Now this boy was picked up by the *Rakshasas.* One day some of the women went to bathe and found a pot flowing down the river. There attention was drawn to it by the cries of a child. They caught hold of the pot and brought it on the bank. They found in it a very beautiful boy, only a few days old. They took up the child and brought it home. Since then *Mihir* became one of the *Rakshasa* boys and grew up under the fostering care of the women who found him in the river. When *Khanâ* and *Mihir* both grew up to marriageable age they were married.

But although we cannot trace the parentage of *Khanâ*; we know whose son *Mihir* was. He was the son of *Barâha,* one of the nine great scholars, who were attached to the court of *Bikramâditya,* the most celebreated king of ancient India. Astrology was the forte of *Barâha* and when a son was born to him, he sat down to calculate the length of his life. He found that it was only ten-years.* When he found it, it pained him very much,—but he thought, it would be best to remove the child now, than to bring him up and to see him die when he would be ten years old. He put the child into an earthern pot and

* It was a mistake of his, it was not ten, but one hundred.

let it float down the river. We know how the child was found and brought up.

After marriage *Khana* and *Mihir* wished to come amongst their own people. They got permission from their *Rakshasa* friends and started towards the Aryan country. A woman was despatched with them with the books on Astrology. She was instructed to deliver them the books on coming to the border of the *Rakshasa* land, if she found that they were not adepts in it and still required to study it;—if otherwise, she was to bring the books back.

On coming to the frontier, the woman saw a cow in labour-pain. "*Mihir*," asked she, "tell me of what colour the calf of this cow would be?" "Surely white," replied *Mihir*. But soon the cow gave birth to a black calf. "Well," said the woman, "you can take these books with you. You have still to learn much." Thus saying she went away.

Mihir was very sory to find that after so many years' hard labour he could not do an easy calculation. "Well," cried he, "if so many years' labour could not make me an astrologer, what these books could do?" He took up the books and flung them into the river. *Khanâ* was at a distance, but when she saw the mad act of her husband, she ran towards the river;—but she could save but two out of the three books ; one was lost for ever.*

They arrived at a place, where Raja *Bikramâditya* came on a hunting excursion. *Khanâ and Mihir* knowing him to be a great patron of learning, appeared before him. Finding them great adepts in astrology, the king took them with him and brought them to his capital. He asked *Barâha* to take charge of them and to keep them comfortably in his house. Then the old Pundit found that *Mihir* was none else but his own dear son. How happy he and his wife were to get back their son and with him a daughter-in-law as good, handsome and learned as any could wish for!

Thus they passed their life very happily for a year. *Mihir* was soon recognized as a great astrologer and was much honoured by the king. *Khanâ* was a greater adept in the mysterious Science ; what her husband or her father-in-law could not calculate, she used to do for them. Thus her name spread all over the country and at last reached the ear of the king.

One day Raja *Bikramâditya* asked *Barâha*

* It is said the book on the astronomy of the region under the earth was thus destroyed.

to tell him the total number of the stars. He took one day's time to answer the great king's query. And though he laboured hard he could do nothing of it. It was impossible to say what was the number of the stars. He was very morose and melancholy, alas, at last his great fame and prestige would be gone for ever !

Khanâ asked him the cause of his uneasiness, and when told she smiled and said, "Father, you need not be anxious for it. I shall calculate and find it out." So she did. The next morning *Barâha* surprised the whole court by telling the king the exact number of the stars. The king did not believe that it was his work ; he pressed him to say who calculated it. The Pundit was obliged to say, "My Liege, it was done by my daughter-in-law." The king expressed his greatest satisfaction and ordered that *Khanâ* would be the tenth jewel of his royal court.

Barâha was thunderstuck. How could his daughter be brought to the court ! She was a woman and a married woman,—she would be an outcast, if she would come to the court. Death was preferable to such indignity and disgrace ! He came to his house resolving to cut off the tongue of *Khanâ*,—the tongue that had brought ruin upon his family. He asked his son *Mihir* to do it ;—

both the husband and the wife knew through their knowledge of astrology that such would be her fate. *Khanâ* widened her mouth with her usual lovely smiles and *Mihir* cut off her tongue. She died a few hours after as happy as ever.

RANI SANJUCTA.

[1]

JOY Chandra was the king of Kanauj in the province of Oudh, when the fearful king Muhammad Ghori invaded India. Beautiful and accomplished *Sunjucta* was his daughter,—she was the Princess Royal of *Kanyakubja*. She was the most handsome, most accomplished and most admired of all the princesses of India; and many a prince from far and near sighed to secure her hands. But *Joychandra* intended to hold a *Syambhar* and to invite all the chiefs and potentates to come to the assembly, so that according to the custom of yore his beloved daughter might make her own choice. He held a great *Rajshuya Jagma*, in which he asked the neighbouring kings and potentates to appear and to pay him homage. *Joychandra* was a mighty ruler ; he was feared by all and respected by the warriors. All came except *Prithiraj,* the king of Delhi. *Joychandra* took mortal offence ; he had an effigy of the proud king made and placed at the door of the assembly room, where he had it dressed in the garb of a menial.

In this assembly room the Princess was asked to appear and make her choice of a husband. Princess *Sanjucta* appeared in the assembly of princes,—a beautiful garland was round her neck, glittering in gold and purple and smiling her ever sweet smile. All was silent and expectant, —even the drop of a pin might be heard through the length and breadth of that large assembly. She stood like a queen in that great conclave of royal princes and ruling heads; she surveyed them all. She moved on and passed by all the royal princes, one after the other, till she came to the door of the room where stood the effigy of the great *Prithiraj.* She did not look back ; she did not see what the assembly said or did. She took up the garland from her neck and placed it round that of the mud effigy of the king of Delhi. There was a great uproar all over the place; king *Joychandra* grew mad with anger ; the insult was too much to be endured; it sent him to the highest pitch of fury. He ordered his ministers to send the girl at once to prison and keep her there, till she would repent for her insolence and folly. She was instantly seized and removed; the assembled chiefs and potentates went away to their own countries.

The news reached Delhi. King *Prithiraj* was informed of what had happened at *Kanauj* and what the royal princess had done and what punishment she had received for her bold behaviour. As soon as he heard all this, he immediately ordered his army to be ready in order to march towards the kingdom of *Joyhcandra.* He came;—*Joy chandra* went out; there was a great battle, in which the king of Kanauj was defeated and his capital was taken. The Princess was brought out of the dungeon and taken away to Delhi; *Prithiraj* married her in all pomp and grandeur.

Joychandra dared not go to war with the king of Delhi. He forgot not the insult and burnt with ever-lasting vengeance. Soon after this sad family broil, the dread king of the Musulmans, Muhammad came to India and moved on and on like an all-destroying tornado scattering ruin and havock all around. The temples were pulled down, the gods and goddesses were destroyed, the villages were looted and burnt, poor women in hundreds were taken prisoners and were given to lustful soldiers to be made ever-lasting slaves. Dishonour and death danced in demoniac merriment over the land through which Muhammad and his hordes passed. There was no time to lose,—any how these monsters must be punished and sent back to their mountain homes. King *Prithiraj* called all the chiefs and potentates of India to arms to defend the honour of their women, the sanctity of their temples and liberty of their country. All hastened towards Delhi to join his standard, except *Joychandra*, who kept himself aloof sullen and revengeful, forgetting all that is good and noble in human heart. But to his credit it must be said that he had the sufficient sense of self-honour to stand aloof and not to join the enemy.

There was a great battle fought between the Hindus and the Mahomedans on the plains of *Tirauri*. Muhammad and his army were defeated, Muslmans were cut down in hundreds and the Ghori king barely escaped with his life.

[2]

But this was too much for *Joychandra* to endure. All success of *Prithiraj* was gall and worm-wood to him. He could suffer and endure all, except the glory of his arch-enemy. Revenge hurled him down to the lowest abyss of sin and enmity; it made him commit most foul and shameful deeds. He sent emissary to the kingdom of Muhammad and invited him to come again to India. He promised him help; he declared his intention of openly joining him. He asked his emissary to inform him that he had broken the coalition of the chiefs and *Prithiraj* had been left to fight his battle alone. The Musulman king soon again collected a great army and hastened towards Delhi. *Joychandra* marched with joy and pride; for at last the great ambition of his life was going to be crowned with success.

Joychandra did not stop by simply calling in the greatest enemy of India in order to suffer the country to be looted and dishonoured, he applied all his intelligence and diplomacy to engender internal dissensions amongst the ruling chiefs. Thus *Prithiraj* found himself forgotten by all his brother-kings,—all kept aloof and left him to fight his own battle; miscreant *Joychandra* openly joined the enemy and marched with his army to welcome him.

He had encamped his army on the banks of the Jumuna and was daily expecting the approach of the Mahomedan hordes. He was alone in his tent dreaming of the joy that would accrue from the defeat of *Prithiraj*. Oh, nothing like enjoying the sweets of revenge! A soldier came and saluted him saying, "Maharaj, a young soldier from the enemy's camp prays to have an interview." "A young soldier!" mused the king, "Ah! a young soldier from the enemy's camp! What does he want?" "An ambassador;" replied the soldier, and he added, "therefore we have allowed him to pass through our ranks and I have brought him to your Majesty's camp." "Bring him here; no,—you better wait outside and send him here," said the king and rose to take his sword.

A soldier came; he saluted him and fell on his knees. "What do you want?" asked *Joychandra* in astonishment. "Father," said *Sanjucta* in disguise, "I have come to pray for your blessings. I am going to fight for my country and I must meet the enemy with your blessings, for without paternal blessings my success will not be assured." *Joychandra* stood like a statue for five minutes; then he tried to say something, but he stopped and looked at his daughter intently for five minutes more. Then he said, "You are the cause of all this! Go away, it is too late." "Father, father, dear father," cried the princess and clasped the feet of the king with her arms, "Do kindly look to your country,—look to the poor and helpless women that will be dishonoured, to the gods and godesses that will be demolished, to the holy temples that will be defiled, to the"——" Stop girl," said the king, "go away. It is too late." "Will all my prayers be in vain!" said the Princess and rose from her suppliant posture. She turned towards her father like an enraged lioness and said, "You have to murder your own daughter before you can bring shame and disgrace to the manes of our great fore-fathers. Shame, father, shame! Oh, heaven, *you* join the Musalmans and sell your country to them!"

Joychandra quickly left the tent and passed orders that the soldier that had come to see him, should be taken care of, so that he might safely reach his own camp. Then he took horse and rode away to the direction of the Mohamedan camp. *Sanjucta* waited for a quarter of an hour and then came out and searched for her father. But he was not to be found. Then she quietly passed through the camp and returned to her husband.

Prithiraj knew that there was no chance of success this time. *Sanjucta* knew too. The husband and wife met and bade each other a loving farewell. She went away to Delhi to save the honour of the women and *Prithiraj* remained in the battle-field to see that his men might not disgrace themselves. " My dear wife," said the king, "rest assured, I shall not disgrace myself by leaving the field till I am alive and I am sure each and every one of my soldiers would do the same." " Dear husband," replied the queen, "that is why I leave you. If I do not go back to Delhi, they will not be able to save themselves;—poor things,—they will be confused and terror-stricken. But rest assured when my father with his friends reaches Delhi, they will not find a living woman in the city."

[3]

Some months passed before the hostile armies met in a deadly combat. Both parties were unwilling to begin the hostilities. They were so strong that both parties were afraid of each other, and looked at each other defiantly from a safe distance. *Prithiraj* passively waited the attack and his enemies took some months to get themselves ready to attack him. And all these long months, there in Delhi lived *Sanjucta* only on water and bread, observing the strictest asceticism. Her noble example was followed by all the women of the city ;

they were all ready to die at a moment's notice. From the queen down to the beggar woman they all prayed day and night for the victory,—prayed to their gods and goddesses to save their country's liberty and to protect their beloved idols and temples.

At last the battle was faught. As it was expected the whole Hindu army was totally annihilated; none surrendered, none asked for grace; each and every one of them faught till he was dead. The dead body of the king was found underneath a heap of faithful retainers,—all covered with innumerable wounds. A complete victory was gained by Muhamad of Ghori and he congratulated *Joychandra* on his unexpected good fortune. But some how *Joychandra* was disappointed; he thought he would be very happy by the fall of his great enemy, but now when it did happen, he became very very miserable.

They buried and burnt their dead and marched towards Delhi. When they reached the fallen city, they found a big funeral pyre smouldering down in front of the Palace. All was at an end. *Sanjucta* had entered the burning pyre as a queen enters her royal court. She had been followed by the ladies of the royal household; all the women of the city had followed her noble example. The men of Delhi had fallen in the field of battle,—to defend the liberty of their country and the women had fallen into the pyre,—to save their honour.

Joychandra felt the bitterest pangs of remorse; but alas, it was too late. He soon gathered his men and marched away to his kingdom. And readers of history know that the very next year his kingdom was invaded by his so-called friend Muhamad of Ghori;—he was defeated and beheaded and his kingdom was annexed to the Mahamedan Empire of Delhi.

PADMINI.

[1]

IN the beginning of the 12th century the Mewer kingdom was the most powerful sovereignty in the north of India. *Chetor*, its capital, was the most important city in the historic land of Rajputana. It was the centre of all heroism, all civilisation, all that was grand, sublime and beautiful. At the time of which we are speaking, Maharana Lakshman Sing was the ruling sovereign,—but he was a minor; consequently the government was vested in his uncle Bhima Sing. None was so great in arms or in council; never was the Mewer kingdom so benignly ruled;—there was peace and contentment all over the kingdom and Bhima Sing was loved, admired and adored.

But sooner than it was expected, the peace and happiness of the people of Mewer came to an end. The terrible king of the Moslems, Allauddin was over-running the whole of Northern India. He was looting cities and towns, demolishing temples and shrines and massacring the old and the young. In his destructive mood he came near the great Mewer kingdom. He found it defended by a most heroic and powerful race. He was rather unwilling to risk his reputation by invading such a powerful kingdom ;—he was at the point of turning the course of his stupendous army to some other direction, when he heard of the common, unsurpassed and unmatched beauty of *Padmini*, the wife of the regent, Bhima Sing. Lust and avarice were his ruling passions ; he stopped and encamped. He first tried secretly ;—he sent spies into the city, and bribed women of bad characters to negotiate with the *Rani*, but he was very much mistaken in his estimation of *Padmini*, who was a woman far beyond his conception and moral ideas. Failing in this, he marched out with his great army and laid siege to the great city of *Chitor*. He met with a hot reception ; arms met with arms ; the heroic sons of

Mewer were as firm as the rocks on which their castle stood. There were hard fightings,—there were night attacks and day skirmishes,—Rajputs were resolved upon death or victory,—Moslems on the other hand were determined to conquer the country. Allauddin had taken a solemn vow that he would secure *Padmini* or die in the rocky lands of Rajputana.

Days after days passed, months after months rolled away,—still *Chitor* stood the siege of the great Moslem forces; but the number of her defenders got thinner and thinner every day,—the Moslems won by their numerical strength. Bhima Sing defended *Chitor* to the last, but he could no longer retain her, for a very large number of his soldiers had been killed or wounded. He was at last obliged to negotiate with the Moslem invader; he asked for peace and offered gold to buy it. It pained him,—death was preferred to such humility,—but noble Bhima Sing submitted to all for the sake of his dear and beloved subjects. But, alas, the monster of iniquity, cruel and lustful Allauddin rejected all offers. He sent words that there was but one means by which the Rajputs could get peace and it was to deliver up *Padmini* to his lust. The Rajputs as a body rejected this most insulting proposal and resolved to fight to the last. So fightings were renewed and the siege continued.

About a year and a half past, still Allauddin could not take possession of the Rajput capital; still the Rajputs withstood the attacks of his vast hordes as the rocks withstand the continual dashing waves of a tempestuous ocean. The great Moslem invader grew tired of fighting,—he became half-willing to let the Rajputs and their *Chitor* alone,—but he could not honourably retire without once more trying to get possession of *Padmini.* He offered peace; he sent messengers to Bhima Sing to propose that if he could only once allow Allauddin to see his wife, he would very gladly make peace with the Rajputs and retire with his army. The Rajputs were at the last strait; they held a council of war, and it was finally decided that if the Moslem would agree to see the reflection of the Rani on a looking-glass, there was no harm to allow him to do it; but he must come into the fort with only a few retainers. Allauddin agreed, a day was fixed, and all fightings ceased. At the appointed day and time Allauddin came and saw *Padmini* through a looking-glass. He expressed his greatest satisfaction, made many apologies to Bhima Sing for his invasion of the country and promised to be a friend of *Chitor* till his death. "My friend," said he, "if I knew what a brave race your Rajputs are and what a noble and glorious man their Regent is, I would never have crossed arms with them and would have courted their friendship. I am extremely honoured by getting your friendship. Henceforth all enmity between the Musulmans and the Rajputs ceases for ever." He took up the hand of Bhima Sing and said, "I have one prayer to make before we part. I am sure you will not disappoint me. Come to my camp to-morrow and honour it with your presence." The noble, the truthful, the honest and straight-forward Rajput Chief accepted his invitation and promised to go to his camp.

With only a few attendants Bhima Sing set out from his fort and rode towards the Moslem camp. But the treacherous Musulman kept hidden some hundreds of soldiers on his way to the camp. They lay in ambuscade behind a jungle. As Bhima Sing and his party came near them, they rushed out. Before the Rajputs could make any attempt to defend themselves, they were all taken prisoners. There was great joy all over the Moslem camp,—there were dismay and confusion within the city of *Chitor*. It was tenfold increased when a messenger from the Moslem camp approached the fort and cried, "O you Rajputs, know the command of our king. If you do not forthwith deliver your *Padmini Rani* to our general and king, Bhima Sing will be killed and fightings will be renewed."

Rana Lakshman Sing was a boy,—so were the twelve sons of Bhima Sing. When he was taken prisoner, the command of the army fell on Gora Sing, the brother of *Padmini;* but the Government was managed by *Padmini*, the wife of the Regent. She called all the Sirdars, generals and princes to a council and consulted how to rescue the Regent and defend the city. The brave *Rani* offered to go over to the enemy's camp. A stratagem was played and the Moslems fell into the snare.

A messenger was despatched to the Musulman king with the offer of peace. The *Rani* offered to go to the king, provided her husband was safely delivered to the city. But as her innumerable maids would not leave her till the last, he must allow them also to come to his camp to bid her their last farewell. Allauddin's joy knew no bounds. At last he was going to get *Padmini*, whose unmatched beauty had made him mad! He agreed to all her proposals and asked the messenger to hasten back and send their *Rani* as soon as possible.

Padmini came out o the fort in a palankeen. She was followed by seven hundred palankeens,—carried by sturdy Rajputs with arms hidden under their clothes. Within each palankeen were two Rajput warriors armed to the teeth. They were accompanied by their general *Gora* and his son *Badal,* a boy of only twelve years of age. But the Moslems suspected nothing;—they welcomed the *Rani* in royal state and allowed the seven hundred closed palankeens to pass into their camp.

[2]

Allauddin hurried to meet *Padmini,* but she said from her closed palankeen, "O mighty Sultan, I have come to be yours,—I shall never again see my husband. Allow me to see him once for the last time." The king found no reasonable objection to it and ordered the palankeen to be carried to the place where Bhima Sing was kept prisoner."

Two bold Rajputs had assumed the garb of Musulmans and entered the Moslem camp night before. They had come with two of the best horses and passed unrecognised into the camp. They had instructions to keep the horses ready near the tent in which the Rana was kept a prisoner. The palankeen neared the Rana's tent,—*Padmini* anxiously waited for the men and found them standing almost at the door of.it. Her anxiety was gone and she entered the tent.

Bhima Sing was astonished to find his wife in the enemy's camp. " What is this ?" exclaimed he, "why are *you* here ?" " Hush," said she, " No time to lose. Arm yourself. There are horses outside the tent. All arrangements have been made for our escape. Come, dear husband, come." Rana Bhima Sing and *Padmini* came out of the tent so suddenly that the guards could not get time to stop them. Like lightnings they rushed towards the horses; in a twinkling of an eye, they got upon the fiery steeds and disappeared. The guards raised a hue and cry,—there were confusion and alarm all over the camp, in the midst of which the Rajputs came out of their palankeens and attacked the Moslems. Thus the Musulmans could get neither time nor opportunity to pursue the Rajput chief and his brave wife. Their flight was covered by the Rajputs and they rode away to their city in safety.

Here in the camp fought the Rajputs like enragad lions when at bay. They were soon encircled by hordes of Musulman soldiers, but they fell as only heroes fall on the field of battle. General *Gora* fell in the thickest of fighting and the command was at once taken up by his son, *Bâdal*. Who would not fight when he sees a boy only 12 years old fighting before him, rushing amongst the enemies, and killing them as a young and ferocious tiger kills deer? The Rajputs fought till they were annihilated. They went out to give opportunity to their *Rani* to rescue their beloved Ruler,—they went out to die to save their chief and leader. They died,—none returned to the city to tell the tale. But they had killed half of the Moslem soldiers, and entirely destroyed Allauddin's camp. More than twelve hundred years have rolled away in the unknowable space of time, but still the names of boy *Badal* and his Rajput soldiers are sung in rural ballads and city songs.

[3]

After the escape of Bhima Sing and the fall of brave Badal, both parties became desperate. The Rajputs determined to exterminate the Moslems or to die in the attempt;—the Musalmans resolved to take possession of *Chitor* or to die on the battle-field. But alas, the Rajputs had little hope of success. Bhima Sing had seen a vision,—a cry of *Mai Bhuka ho* (I am hungry) was heard by him night and after night; the presiding goddess of *Chitor* had appeared before him and told him that unless she would drink the blood of twelve royal heads, her thirst would not be quenched. Yes, one after another eleven sons of Bhima Sing had sallied forth to destroy the Musalmans and, one after another they were all killed. There would be but one struggle more,—it was the last and final attempt of the Rajputs to drive away the Musulmans from the gate of their city. There was no hope of success, for their number had been reduced to hundreds, whereas the Musalmans were thousands. But they had all determined to die in order to defend their country. They knew they would die, but they must save at least one scion of the royal house, so that he might again establish a new *Chitor* kingdom. The youngest son of Bhima Sing was saved; the boy was given to a maid servant; she left *Chitor* with the boy, and went into jungle. The Moslems did not know that one of the Rajput Princes had been removcd from their deadly grasp.

They all,—each and every one of the city, except decripit old men and helpless children, went out to fight with the enemy under the command of their chief Bhima Sing. We need not describe the battle, in which one side was resolved to sell their lives dearly and in which they were determined to die, killing as many of the enemies as possible. From morning to evening the battle raged ;—by the evening there was not a single Rajput alive ;—but Allauddin's stupendous army was almost exterminated.

In the evening when the sad news reached the city, by the order of their *Rani Padmini*, the Rajput women made a large funeral pyre at the centre of the city. She came out with all her maids and was followed by all the women of the city. Fire was set to the funeral pile,—soon the destructing element raged and foamed ;—the fire lighted up the whole city, showing its deadly aspect. *Padmini* followed by the women took seven turns round the pyre and then jumped into the blazing element. Her example was instantly followed by others. When Allauddin reached the city, he found all was at an end ; the fire of the pile was slowly going down.

He won the battle and he conquered *Chitor*, but he found ruins for his possession and decripit old men and helpless children for his booty.

THE RANI OF ARGAL.

THERE was a Hindu Principality in Argal, near the modern Buxar in Behar. The name of the chief was Goutam and the heroine of our story was his wife. He refused to pay the tribute to the Mahomedan Emperor of Delhi and the Governor of Oudh was ordered to march against him. He found the brave Raja more than his match, for the imperial troops were defeated with very great slaughter. The remnant returned with haste and fear, while the Raja marched back to his castle and proclaimed a feast in honour of the victory.

On the day of the full moon the Rani was filled with fear, for unless she could bathe in the holy

Ganges disaster would surely visit her home. But the banks of the Ganges were in the possesion of their foes. The *Rani* thought over the matter in solitude and resolved to slip out with her maids and hurry down to the bathing ghaut at Buxar, only a few miles off. She could go *incognito* and hurry back again to the castle.

With eager steps they went on their way in the darkness of the night. When the morning broke they found themselves near the

> 'Mother of mighty rivers
> Adored by saint and sage ;
> The much-loved peerless Ganga,
> Famous from age to age.'

With swift steps and glad heart. they hastened forward and arrived at the ghaut. They performed the sacrifices of the full moon and bathed in the holy water. Everything had so far passed off quietly, but it was scarcely to be expected that such a lady could visit the ghaut without attracting notice. Very soon it reached the ear of the Governor of Oudh whose camp was hard by. He soon learnt that the lady was none other than the Rani of Argal. Immediately the order was passed that the Rani should be captured.

As the Rani with her maids was returning to the castle they were surrounded by Moslem soldiers. It is better to describe the state of her mind in the words of a poet,

'The fear was in her bosom,
  The Rani shed no tear;
And her eye resentful sparkled,
  As the enemy drew near.

She stood there brave and scornful,
  Her maids by her side;
And with undaunted calmess
  The Ajodhya's chief defied.'

Each and every one of these brave women had a dagger underneath their clothes. They drew them out and prepared to cut their way to their castle. But when the Rani found that it was an impossible task, she cried out,—

" Are there no Hindu clansmen,
  No Hindu brother here,
To whom a Hindu mother
  And a Hindu wife is dear?

If such there be, arouse ye,
  Stand forth, stand forth to aid,
By the gods I adjure you,
  My cause on you is laid."

Scarcely had these burning words left the lips of the Rani, when two brave men, named *Abhai Cand*, and *Nirbhai Cand* with a few followers sprang upon the enemies with a shout. In a few moments they cut their way to the side of the Rani and her maids, who were stoutly defending themselves against the grasp of the ruffians around. With a mighty effort they opened a path through the crowd and with the ladies in their midst they tried to reach the castle. But it was a desperate struggle, every foot of the way had to be won at the sword's point. Brave *Nirbhai* fell mortally wounded and with him fell many more. But soon succour came. The news reached the Chief of Argal who hastened with his men to rescue his wife. When the Mahommedans saw him and his brave men, they turned and fled.

> "But all rejoiced to see her,
> And with one voice did tell
> How the Rani and her maidens
> Had fought so brave and well."

The Chief of Argal was so pleased with the bravery of *Abhai* that he gave him his daughter in marriage ;—and what became the fate of the cowardly Governor? Friend and foe upbraided him for his cowardly attack on the Rani of Argal,

> "When white with age
> Still then he bore the shame,
> That he had wielded weapon
> Against a noble dame."

KARUM DEVI.

KARUM Devi was the daughter of the chief of the Mahils, whose seat was at a place called Aureent. Her father was not a ruler or a potentate, but as she was beautiful and accomplished, the Ruler of Mundore offered to marry her and his proposal was accepted. A formal betrothal was made and the day was fixed for the happy nuptials.

But all these happy arrangements were overturned by the arrival of a stranger in the court of the chief of Aureent. He was a desert chief, named Sadoo,—a man of undaunted courage and chivalrous knight errantry. He was a terror of the country and carried his raids far and wide. The chief of Aureent had often heard of his exploits, but he had never seen him. So on one occasion when Sadoo was returning to his desert home after a fray, he invited him to his castle and asked him to partake of his hospitalities. The invitation was accepted and Sadoo stopped for a week at Aureent.

Karum Devi saw the young hero, whose manly form and martial fame completely won her heart. She listened to his wonderful stories of adventure and lost her heart to the gallant hero. But her unhappy love brought miseries and misfortunes on her family. She was already betrothed and her love towards Sadoo resulted in her death.

She opened her heart to her hand-maidens,—they told it to her mother. She on her part disclosed the matter to her husband. The chief of Aureent knew not what to do. How could he cancel the engagement with the Ruler of Mundore? Surely he would take it to be a great insult;—there would be war, carnage and bloodshed. No,—by no means he could plunge his country into a bloody campaign for the foolish whims of a wayward girl! *Karum* must not think of others,—she must marry Mundore or marry none.

But is there a man who can ever act against the wish of his better half! The ladies became victorious as they always are all over the world. The chief had to submit to their will. That the happiness of the daughter should stand over all other considerations, was the argument of the mother and it carried weight. A messenger was despatched to the father of Sadoo with the proposal of marriage. We need not say, the offer was most gladly accepted and the bridegroom started for Aureent with seven hundred stalwart followers. The nuptials were solemnised in great pomp and the happy pair started for their desert home.

The Ruler of Mundore took severe offence at the behaviour of the chief of Aureent. He could not prevent the marriage, but he was resolved upon vengeance. He collected four thousand soldiers and planted himself in the path which Sadoo and his wife had to take.

Merrily went the bridal party on its way to the desert home, fearing no evil and suspecting no disaster. But they soon found that their way was blocked by the army of the disappointed and aggrieved lover. If they would win their way home, they must fight.

But the Ruler of Mundore, like a gallant foe, scorned the advantage of numbers. He challenged his foe to a single combat. A series of single combats ensued with all the forms of chivalry. The two chiefs stood looking on, expressing their approval of the bravery and skill of their followers.

At last the gallant Sadoo prepared himself for action,—the Mundore chief was already impatient to meet him. Sadoo came to his wife and bade her farewell. She buckled his sword and said, "Dear husband, I shall witness your deed. If you' fall, I shall follow you in death." Again and again he was challenged to the combat;—but though she said bold and brave words yet she could not say good bye to him. At last he extricated himself from her loving grasp and went forth to meet the Ruler of Mundore.

They met, each wishing to yield to his rival the first blow. It was at length struck by Sadoo on the neck of the Mundore prince. With the rapidity of lighting it was returned and *Karum Devi* saw the steel descend on the head of her lover. Both fell on the ground, Sadoo in the agonies of death, but the chief of Mundore only fainted from the loss of blood.

There was great mourning over the slain,—but there was no tear in the eyes of *Karum Devi*. She assumed the command of her husband's army; she took the sword of her husband which lay by him; and before she could be prevented she severed her left arm from the shoulder. She gave command that it should be conveyed to her father-in-law in the fastness of the desert. "Tell him," said she, "such was his daughter. She was not unworthy to be the wife of his brave son." Then she ordered her attendants to cut off her right arm and carry it to her father. "Tell him also," said she, "that his daughter died as the woman of the brave Mahil race should die." Finding her attendant unwilling to carry out her orders, she turned towards them like a lioness and pealed forth, "Do you dare disobey your general's order?" A man advanced from the rank and said, "Lady, we have not forgotten discipline. We hesitated because we admire and respect you. But let it not be said that you are not accepted as our general and therefore we refused to carry out your orders. With your permission and under your command, I cut off your arm." *Karum Devi* stood like a statue and saw both of her arms chopped off.

She then prepared herself for the flames. A funeral pyre was erected on the field of battle just where her husband had fallen. Calmly and silently she gave herself up with him to the devouring flames, amidst loud acclamations of both the armies.

TARA BAI.

[1]

THODA was a small kingdom in Rajputana. In the beginning of the sixteenth century one *Suratan* was its chief and ruler;—but he was not strong enough to defend his country from the attacks of the powerful armies of the Musulman Emperor of Delhi. They came in hordes and hemmed him in;—he appealed to the neighbouring chiefs and his sovereign the Maharana Sangram Sing of Mewer, to come or to send armies to his help. But alas, each and every one of the Rajput chiefs, from the Maharana down to the pettiest Takur were all auxious to look after their own kingdoms,—for they were all in the same plight. Each and every one of them was attacked by the Musulmans and each and every one of them was engaged in defending his own country. Thus none came to *Suratan's* help,—he did what was possible to be done to defend his country,—but finally he was driven out of his kingdom and his most beloved *Thoda* passed into the hands of the victorious Moslems.

He retired with his only daughter *Tara* to *Bidnore*, a place near *Chitor*, the capital of the Mewer kingdom. There lived he a life of retired ease, but he never forgot his kingdom of *Thoda* and its poor oppressed people. What could he do without soldiers, without means, and without money or arms! The king of *Chitor* whose vassal he was, could do nothing for him,—for he himself was beset with the armies of Delhi.

But *Suratan* never gave up hope to recover his lost kingdom. He fondly hoped that time would surely come when he would have an opportunity of regaining his *Thoda*. His hope rested on his most beloved and loving daughter *Tara*. He had no son;—but he brought up *Tara* as a boy and gave her all the training of a soldier. From her early age *Tara* had learnt to ride horses, to handle swords and to use bows and arows. She was a heroine in all its shades. Her beauty was exquisite,—there was none so handsome in Rajputana.

She was endowed with all the qualifications of a great lady,—but at the same time she was as bold as a lioness,as spirited as a tigress, and as courageous and skillful in war as the best of the Rajputs. More than once did *Suratan* attempt to regain his kingdom, and on each occasion *Tara* fought by his side.

Suratan fondly hoped that though unfortunately he did not get an opportunity to regain his kingdom, yet the training that he was giving to his daughter would make her quite capable to regain it, provided he would die without getting back his lost kingdom. The education that he had given her would make her quite capable of doing it, in case he would die before he regained his kingdom. He resolved that none but the man who would be able to drive the Musulmans from his kingdom of *Thoda* would get thehand of his most beautiful and accomplished daughter *Tara*. The fame of the matchless beauty and accomplishments of *Tara* spread all over Rajastan; many a prince grew eager to get possession of the beautiful girl,—but *Suratan* was inexorable.

One after another proposed and was rejected, till the third son of the Rana of Mewer, *Joymalla,* proposed to marry the princess. *Suratan* was a vassal of the Rana, it was an honour to him to get his daughter married to the son of the great man,—but his patriotism rose above all considerations. "No, Prince," said he, "I can marry my daugher to none else, but to him who would be able to regain my *Thoda*." *Joymalla* was proud, vain and vicious; he was a coward and a base debauchee; he sneered at *Suratan*,—cut vulgar jokes at his beautiful daughter and boasted that the position of *Suratan* would be soon so low that he would be glad to hire out his daughter to the groom of his stable. *Suratan* could no longer endure; he drew out his sword and before he could be prevented, he beheaded the young prince.

The Rana was as noble as the great ruler of the brave and heroic race of Rajputs should have been. When the news of his son's encounter with *Suratan* reached him, he said, "Well, he deserved it. He was the curse of my family and as he attempted to do which no Rajput would have done, I pardon *Suratan* for killing him."

[2]

Now there was another son of the Rana, named *Prithi Rai*. He incurred his father's displeasure and was ordered to live out of the jurisdiction of the Mewer kingdom. But on the death of *Joymalla* the Rana recalled his banished son and restored to him his status as a prince of the blood. His return was welcomed by the people of *Chitor*, for he was the best of all the princes. None was so handsome, none was so courageous, none was so able a soldier as he. Surely amongst all the Rajput Princes he was the fittest man to be the husband of the young princess. If there was any man in Rajputana who deserved to be possessed of the hand of *Tara*, it was Prince *Prithi Rai* of *Chitor*. The Rana was willing,—*Surutan* was also willing to see him his son-in-law; *Tara* herself was in deep love with *Prithi* and *Prithi* with *Tara*,—but alas, there was a great obstacle in their way to happiness! There was the solemn vow of *Surutan* that none but he who would be able to regain *Thoda* would get his daughter for his wife.

Prithi Rai determined to make an attempt. Well, it was all the same,—to die in the attempt or to live without his beloved *Tara*. It was better to die with glory instead of living in ignomy and without *Tara*. He collected two hundred best Rajput horsemen and prepared to march towards *Thoda*. We need not say, *Tara*, notwithstanding all protest, accompanied her affianced.

They came near *Thoda* and encamped under

the cover of a dense forest. *Prithi Rai* intended to surprise the Mahomedans in the day of their annual great festival of *Maharam*, which is celebrated in memory of the murder of the martyr Husein. On this occasion the Musulmans become mad with excitement and burn with religious enthusiasm. This is the day on which they grow as fearful as demoms; but this was the day on which *Prithi Rai* determined to attack them.

Early in the evening two horsemen, followed by another, entered the citadel of *Thoda*. The first two were *Prithi Rai* and *Tarabai*, the third horseman was the chief of *Sengarh*, the most intimate and dearest friend of *Prithi Rai*. He had left his men with instructions to advance towards the fort. The Rajput cavalry advanced silently and under cover of the hills came at the foot of the citadel. There they lay in waiting as silent and motionless as so many statues. In the meanwhile within the fort had the three heroic souls already began their bloody business. They began to kill whomever they could lay hand upon. There was soon alarm and confusion all over the fort,—people ran in dismay;—soldiers unarmed and undressed ran in all directions,—the great drum was beaten,—and the door of the citadel was shut up.

Prithi Rai expected all this; he knew he

could not surprise the Mahomedans, if he went with all his men. The sounds of the horse's hoops would be heard by the people in the fort long before he could reach its gate;—the door of it would be soon shut up and the soldiers would hurl upon his exposed men all sorts of missiles. This was the reason why he entered the fort unattended by his men, for their arrival drew no attention and when they attacked the Mahomedans all people's attention was naturally centered upon them;—all came rushing towards them. Getting the opportunity of coming unnoticed to the fort his men rushed forward. Here the Prince ran in the fort towards the gate, opened it and allowed the Rajputs to rush into the fort. As previously arranged everything was carried to perfection. The door was opened and *Prithi Rai's* brave Rajputs rushed into the fort and began to butcher the surprised and confused Musulmans. The Mahomedan soldiers tried to rally round, but their attempt failed and they began to fall like leaves under the swords of the Rajputs. *Tara* fought by the side of her husband and felled many of the enemies of her country and the oppressers of her people. By evening victory was complete; three fourths of the Mahomedans lay dead, the rest fled in all directions. *Tara* prevented the

Rajputs to pursue them. "Let them live," said she, "our intention is to regain our kingdom and not to kill them."

We need not say, soon after this victory, *Tara* was married to *Prithi Rai* in great pomp. *Suratan* returned to his ever dear *Thoda,* but soon he retired to *Bidnore* investing *Prithi Rai* and *Tara* with all the power and privileges of Royalty. They lived very happily for a year or two,—when a sad occurrence happened, which brought their happy career to an end.

[3]

When *Prithi Rai* was only twenty three and *Tara* seventeen,—at the very spring of their happy life it was suddenly cut assundar. *Prithi* had a very beloved sister,—she was married to one *Pravu Rai*; this man was a debauchee and tyrant. He ill treated his wife till it grew intolerable to the young Princess to live with him. Finding no other hope of saving herself from persecutions of her husband, she wrote a letter to her chivalrous brother. She knew if there was any body bold enough to redress her wrong, it was her brave brother *Prithi Rai.* She wrote, "My husband's persecutions have become intolerable. He is always drunk and is always engaged in things which cannot be described. Dear brother, if you have any love and feelings for your poor sister, save her from her life of wretchedness and misery."

No sooner *Prithi Rai* received this letter, he at once repaired to the house of *Pravu Rai*;—he reproached him for his cowardice and ignominous conduct. He forced him to place on his head the shoe of his wife as an atonement of his past conduct and a guaruntee for future good behaviour. *Pravu Rai* was afraid of his brother-in-law,—he knew *Prithi Rai* was a man of very strong character; he could kill him if he would chose to do it. He did what he was commanded to do, but he entertained a deadly hatred towards him and determined to wreck severe vengeance upon the man who so publicly insulted him. But he kept his foul intention hidden in his breast, showed the greatest respect for *Prithi Rai* and pressed him to accept his hospitality. Simple and honest *Prithi Rai* never dreamt that his life was aimed at;—he graciously accepted the invitation of his brother-in-law and remained to join him at dinner.

At that fatal dinner, deadly poison was mixed with liquor; and that liquor was given to *Prithi Rai* by *Pravu Rai*,—the young Prince never suspected anything wrong and drank the fatal liquid. When he was leaving the house of his sister, he fell down at the courtyard and fainted. The news soon reached his palace and the palace of his royal father;—his dear wife *Tara* ran to her dying husband,—his old father and brothers came to see what had happened. Every effort was made to save him, but all to no effect. He breathed his last on the lap of his weeping wife amidst the loud lamentations of all the people of *Chitor*.

Was *Tara* going to die with her hutband? Was she going to be a *Sati?* Yes, she was. She was a heroine in her childhood, she was a heroine in her youth,—she was a heroine even in her death. The Maharana, her father-in-law,—*Suratan,* her father, her brothers-in-law, nay all the people of *Chitor*, entreated her to give up the idea of following her husband to death, for she was the most beloved of all. But she stood firm; she asked to be excused in such a tone that people stood silent and dared not repeat their requests and prayers.

A funeral pyre was soon made; the corpse of *Prithi Rai* was placed on it and then began the fearful ceremony of *Sati*. *Tara* went through the thrilling solemnities as calmly as if she was doing nothing extraordinary. When the ceremony was over the Brahmins began to recite the holy texts. Amidst the sounds of music and the din of the crowd, *Tara* walked round and round the pyre and then she ascended it. She lay herself down by the side of her husband and signed to the people to set fire to the funeral pyre. There was great noise,—great uproar,—great sound of drums and gongs; amidst all this the fire was set to the pyre. It soon blazed up and cracked and roared; there was no motion in *Tara's* body,—she lay as motionless as her husband's corpse, perhaps she died before the fire was ablaze.

Within an hour all was at an end. The brave and the heroic *Tara* and her equally chivalrous husband *Prithi* were burnt to ashes. The people of *Chitor* returned home to mourn for the loss,—a loss which they knew would never be replaced.

PANNA.

[1]

SANGRAM SING was one of the most famous kings of Mewer in Rajputana; but he had unconsciously given himself up to one *Banabir*, who was originally a menial servant, but who had been now raised to the high position of the Prime Minister. *Banabir* was not what he was taken for;—he was ambitious as Macbeth and as demoniac as the murderous king of Denmark. But the king trusted him; he placed implicit faith upon his minister; he knew him to be the best of men. And thus when he died, he made *Banabir* the Regent of his son, Udaya Sing, who was then only six years old.

Young Udaya was placed in the charge of a nurse, an ordinary Rajput woman, who was named *Panna*. She brought up the Prince and loved him as much as her own son, who was exactly of his age. She was an old servant of the Royal household, and her mother and grand mother and her ancestors were the servants of the Palace years and years before her. Thus a hereditary love towards the Royal house of Sangram Sing came down to her family from generation to generation; they were ever faithful to their masters and many of her ancestors did extraordinary service to many members of the Royal household; but surely none could be compared with the wonderful act of self sacrifice, patriotism and fidelity of *Panna*.

The uncontrolable ambition of *Banabir* was not satisfied by being the Prime Minister and then the Regent of the finest and the richest of all the kingdoms of Rajasthan; he aspired more. Nothing less than the crown could satisfy him; nothing but usurpation of the throne could make him contented with his lot. A son of a poor maid-servant,—born of a low-family,—having got no education he had become the virtual ruler of Mewer by the unknowable will of Providence—but still he is not contented;—he hankered for the title and honour of the king, not only for himself but for his progeny.

But Prince Udaya Sing was alive; so long the boy breathed, he had no chance of becoming the king of Mewar. Ambition made him a demon as it did many before and after him ;—he determined to murder the boy. He could not trust any man with the execution of the foul deed; if it would ooze out, his own life would not be worth a penny. All the Rajput chiefs, the vassals and allies of the Royal house, would rise in a body and would hunt him down wherever he would take shelter. The deed must be done in secret,—it must be done with his own hands, so that none could know any thing of the foul murder. By cajoling, by flattery and by other fair or foul means in which he was an adept, he knew he would be able to manage the brainless Rajput Chiefs after the deed was once done.

None had penetrated into the black depths of the ambitious heart of the Regent,—none knew what plot he was hatching to remove the only obstacle that lay in his way to the throne. But there was in that extensive royal palace one man who knew what he was. He knew what diabolical thoughts were rolling into his heart,—what foul murder he was contemplating! He was the royal barber ; like *Panna* he was an old servant ; not only he, but his father and grand father and before them their forefathers were all servants of the Royal household. He was never pleased with the sudden rise of *Banabir* from a servant to a Premier and from a Premier to a Regent.

[2]

It was about ten in the night,—*Panna*, after making the Prince and her son sleep, began to sew. All was silent,—not a noise was to be heard anywhere. Suddenly her attention was drawn to hasty footsteps coming towards the door of the Royal nursery. Who could it be that was coming to her at this late hour of the night? Before she could think over the matter, the royal barber came and stood before her. "What is the matter?" asked *Panna*, "Is there any news?" "Yes, news, most fearful news." replied the barber, "the Regent would soon be here to murder the Prince." "As I feared," said *Panna*, "so it would happen! I never loved that man. But we *must* save the Prince." "What could we do?" said the barber, "advise me, *Panna*."

Panna sat silently for a few minutes and then said, "We must remove the Prince from the palace to a place of safety." "Alas!" replied the barber, "the Regent has doubled guards all over the palace. It is his strict order to-night not to allow any one to go out of the palace with a child." "In that case," said *Panna* "we can also outwit him. Get that basket. I shall place the Prince into it and then cover him with the refuses. Carry it as a sweeper carries it, and I am sure no body would ask you anything. Take him to a place of safety." Then *Panna* mentioned the name of a merchant in whose house she asked him to take the Prince. "But," suggested the barber, "he would be soon here and when he would find the Prince gone, he would at once send men all around the city to find him out. It would be impossible to save the Prince." "Well," silently and slowly said *Panna*, "he will not know that the Prince has been removed. My son will be here and I shall place him on the royal bed. If the poor life of my son can save the future king of Mewer, the patron and benefactor of my family from generation to generation,—*Panna* would consider her life blessed." The barber stood silent, he could not utter a word. *Panna* rose and brought the basket. She placed the Prince into it, covered him with refuses and asked the barber to take it on his head and go quietly out of the palace. He was still silent and stood like a statue. *Panna* again asked him to go away with the basket. "What are you doing, *Panna?*" said the barber, "I am doing," replied *Panna*, "what is my duty to do."

The barber was forced to go away; *Panna* placed her son in the royal bed and waited patiently for the murderer. It was twelve O'clock,—the palace was in deep silence; but suddenly *Panna* started up hearing foot-steps,—she turned her head and saw *Banabir* standing in the royal nursery. *Panna* rose up and made him obeisance. "How is the Prince?" asked the Regent and moved towards the bed. "I am anxious for his health," said he, "and I have come to see him." Without seeing who was in the bed he thurst a sharp dagger into the heart of the boy. A piercing shreak pealed through the solitude of night and was echoed and rechoed all over the palace. *Banabir* hastily drew back and lest he be caught red-handed in his foul deed, he fled percipitously to his own rooms.

People rushed into the nursery from all sides; they found *Panna* unconscious in a swoon and the Prince weltering in blood. There were loud lamentations all over the palace; there were sorrow and grief all over the city. When *Panna* recovered, people pressed her to say who murdered the Prince,—

but she thought it best to hide the facts. "A black man," said she, "suddenly entered the room and murdered the prince." Every body was convinced that Prince *Udaya Sing* was murdered and *Panna* left the royal service and went to the place where the young prince was kept hidden. He was kept in the house of a Jain merchant, named *Arhar Sha* and brought up in private till he grew up to be a young Prince.

We need not say that Prince *Udaya* was recognized, *Banabir* was beheaded and the son and the heir of Sangram Sing ascended the throne of Mewer. *Panna* was loved and respected by the king till her death.

THE QUEEN OF GANORE.

(1)

GANORE was a small Hindu State in central India. When one after another the Hindu States were succumbing to the rising tide of the Mahomedan power, little Ganore stood firm and struggled to preserve its independence. The Pathans had been driven out of Delhi,—the Moguls were pouring into India like locusts. They were scattering the Pathans to all directions and were conquering their old possessions. The sturdy Pathan nobles and generals having been pushed to the wall moved off from Delhi and tried new field and pasture. They began to drive away the Hindu chiefs and to take possession of their happy States. Thus one of these *Khans*, having been driven out of Delhi, entered with his followers into the State of Ganore and tried to establish a Mahomedan government there. But he did not find it an easy task. The Raja hastened to oppose his advance and the Pathan general had to fight at every step. Every inch of ground was bitterly contested on both sides,—till fortune smiled on the Moslem banner. The Raja fell fighting and the bravest of his followers shared his fate.

When the news reached Ganore, the Rani did not weep or lament for the death of her beloved husband, but collected as many men as she could get and hastened to replace her husband at the head of the Ganore army, which was still opposing the advance of the victorious Pathans. The Ganore men were much encouraged by her presence,—she was as good a soldier as her brave husband was ; they fought under her as only heroes could fight ;—but all their superhuman efforts were in vain. The Khan had a very large army at his back,—but the Rani had only a few thousand faithful retainers to support her. Their number was daily getting thinner and there was but little hope to save the country from the Mahomedan grasp. But still she fought and did not allow the Pathans to get an inch of ground without a hard contest. Thus having defended five fortresses against the foe, she retreated to her last stronghold on the Narbuda. But scarcely had she left the bark, when the assailants arrived in pursuit. The Pathan cavalry rushed furiously towards the castle, the doors of which were soon closed. Thus many of her heroic men were left outside,—some in the boat, some on the banks on whom the Pathans fell like demons. They were killed, but not before some hundreds of the enemy had kissed the ground.

Within the fort the disheartened defenders were few in number; they were beset by thousands of infuriated Musulmans. But hopeless task as it was, they fought by the side of their queen, till they were overpowered. The Pathans scaled the walls and jumped in hundreds within the fort. There was nothing but to surrender; a messenger was sent to the victor to say that the queen agreed to surrender and prayed to stop the carnage.

[2]

The Khan was exceedingly pleased and received the messenger in all honour. The beauty of the queen was an allurement only secondary to his desire for her country. "Go, Sir," said the Khan, "Go and tell her highness that I am extremely pleased to see her bravery. She is worthy to be a queen. She was a queen and she will remain a queen till I am alive. Tell her that I am her most humble servant. Let her rule over Ganore and over me as her obedient slave." Refusal would have been useless and would have subjected her to instant coercion ; she therefore sent him a message of assent.

"Tell your chief," said she, "that I am exceedingly pleased with his gallant conduct and determination. We ladies always admire bravery and pluck. I admit that he merits my hand. I shall consider it a great honour if the Khan be pleased to accept me as his wife." Then she added, "I wish the nuptials be solemnised on the terrace as it is an old custom of our house. I wish to have two hours' time for preparation as I must appear in a becoming attire which the distinction of my own and his rank demands."

We need not say, all her prayers were granted. The Khan was never so happy in his life and his joy knew no bounds, when a magnificent marriage garb with a necklace set with excellent jewels came from the queen as her present to him. The song of joy had already stifled the discordant voice of war ; merriments had risen on all sides. The

Pathans had thrown off their swords to drink the health of the happy bride. Their chief was mad with impatience to go and see the superb beauty, for whom he longed.

At length the message came,—the Khan in the jewelled garb hastened on the terrace and found the fame had not done justice to her charms. It was a beauty beyond all description. She was sitting on a velvet *devan* and all the ladies of the palace sat apart on some cushions,—which apeared to be some sacks covered with *kinkhubs.* They all held lighted torches in theirs hands and were dressed in their best attire. He was desired to be seated; he had already become a slave and and tried to carry out her slightest wishes with all the grace of courtesy he possessed. He passed some time with her in conversation, and hours were to him were minutes while he gazed on the beauty of the queen. But presently his countenance fell,—he complained of heat. Punkhas and water were brought, but they availed him not. He was in death-agony and began to tear into pieces the bridal garments. The queen rose from her seat and thus addressed him, "Know, Sir, that your last hour is come. The vestments that cover you are poisoned. You had left me no other expedient to escape pollution." The followers of the Khan were horror-struck,—but before they could come to their senses, the Rani sprung from the battlements to the river beneath.

The frantic Pathans rushed towards the ladies; they were sitting on the sacks of gun powder, to which they instantly applied the torches in their hands. A terrible explosion occurred, shaking heaven and earth to its centre; the castle tottered to its foundation, and a volume of smoke rose to the sky; when it was cleared,—nothing was to be seen on the terrace of the Ganore palace, except some mangled human bodies.

The half burnt body of the Khan was found and was buried on the road to Bhopal. He was the founder of the present line of Bhopal Nabobs and strange to say a visit to his grave has the reputation of curing the tertian of that country.

RANI DURGABATI.

[1]

THERE was a small kingdom in central India, named *Gurhmandal.* When every kingdom from the Himalayas to the sea was one after another submitting to superior power of Akbar,—the greatest of all the Emperors of Delhi,—*Gurhmandal* kept her independence and stood like a pillar in the ruins of a great city. And what was more astonishing than the fact that the head of this bold and brave State was but a woman.

Durgabati was the queen of *Gurhmandal.* She was the daughter of *Chandan,* one of the kings of Kanauj in upper India;—she was exceptionally beautiful and accomplished and her father intended to give her in marriage to one of the great chiefs of Rajputana. But *Durgabati* made her own choice,—she fell in love with *Dulapat Sha,* the chief of *Gurhmandal,* and asked him to come to her father's palace. But *Chandan* refused to marry her to *Dalpat,*—who took arms against him. He defeated her future father-in-law and took away his beloved *Durgabati* to his own fortress of *Gurhmandal.*

They lived happily for a few years and *Durgabati* gave birth to a beautiful boy. The child was named *Birnarain.* When the Prince was only three years of age,—*Dulpat* died to the greatest grief of his people and we need not say that it was a great bereavement to poor *Durgabati.*

But she had to put aside her sorrow and grief to take charge of the government on behalf of her child. She had to smile graciously in public and to weep bitterly in private, if she had at all time to weep and mourn for the loss of one who was the dearest and nearest to her heart. However she managed her State as ably and as benignly as her noble husband; she discharged the duties of the charge left to her by her husband to the entire satisfaction of all. She kept the independence of her kingdom entact,—she stood as proudly, though hemmed in by the armies of great Akbar, as her husband used to do.

Governors after governors of the Delhi Empire in charge of Central India applied to the great Emperor for permission to invade the little kingdom of *Gurhmandal*; but Akbar was a man who admired ability. He heard of the fame of the queen of the little State. He heard that she was considered as the mother of the people;—and mother she really was. She caused tanks to be dug all over her State, she built charity-houses, she established beautiful temples, she did a thousand and one thing to make her people happy and contented. The little kingdom of *Gurhmandal* was the best governed State in India; the people were rich, happy and comfortable; the country smiled in rich harvest and flourished in trade and commerce.

Though great Akbar repeatedly refused to grant permission to his governors to conquer *Gurhmandal*, yet he for reasons best known to him yielded at last to the strong representation of Azaf Khan, who was at the time the Musulman Governor of Central India. A strong force was despatched to *Gurhmandal* and Azaf Khan marched to snatch away from the hands of a widowed queen, the kingdom of *Gurhmandal*, for no fault of hers.

Of course *Durgabati* could be no match for great Akbar and his ever renowned army. If he liked he could have deprived her of her kingdom long ago. She was the ruler of a small State,—a smaller and poorer State than the zaigir of the last class *Omrao* of his magnificient court. There was not the least chance for *Durgabati* to defend the liberty of her little kingdom; it was a mad attempt to challenge the forces of Delhi,—it was hoping against hope, but still *Durgabati* stood by her kingdom,—stood by the freedom of her country and tried to defend it or to fall with its downfall.

[2]

She soon collected as many men as she could get;—she was fortunate to raise up an army of eight thousand horse and two thousand elephants;—she was backed by all the people of her kingdom,—all the able-bodied men of *Gurhmandal* hastened to enlist themselves in her army and she herself took the command. There was enthusiasm all over her army,—strong determination to defend the liberty of their country pervaded through them all. They would fight under the command of their brave queen till death.

Azaf Khan never expected that the little kingdom of *Gurhmandal* would be able to master such a strong force. He thought it would be an easy walk and consequently came to invade *Gurhmandal* with an army of five thousand horse only. He thought that 'there would be no fighting whatsoever; there was but a woman at the head of the State! But when he approached *Gurhmandal,* he found out his mistake; but it was too late. He saw that she whom he took to be a weak woman was not a weak woman at all. She herself had commanded her forces and was fully prepared to fight with the Imperial army. He could not now retire with prestige or retreat with safety, he ordered his men to attack the army of the queen.

There was a great battle fought under the walls of *Gurhmandal.* The Imperial army was hopelessly defeated and routed and Azaf Khan escaped barely with his life. There was great joy in *Gurhmandal,* but there was no joy in the heart of *Durgabati,* for she new that her little kingdom would be again attacked by a larger army; she knew that when once the great Mogul had determined to conquer and annex the kingdom, it was not in her power to defend it.

As she expected, within a year and a half a great army was despatched from Delhi to reinforce Azaf Khan and to re-establish the imperial prestige in Central India. Azaf Khan was ordered to conquer the country, to depose the queen and to declare the *Gurhmandal* State as a part of the Delhi Empire.

Durgabati determined to die in defence of her country;—so long she would be alive, none would be able to take possession of the little State,—she again collected a large army, marched out of her fort and gave them battle. Fortune again favoured her; Azaf Khan met with a severe defeat and retreated with a disordered and flying army.

Finding it was not an easy task to conquer *Gurhmandal* by force, the wily Azaf Khan took recourse to diplomacy. He sent spies into her fort,—bribed those that were amenable to bribe,—raised up internal quarrels and dissensions, and disorganised her army by various means and treacherous devices. Thus when on the third time Azaf Khan advanced towards *Gurhmandal, Durgabati* found that fatality had taken possession of her poor State; she found that she had no longer the united support of his soldiers and people; she saw internal dissensions all over the country. She lost heart,—but she knew this would be the destiny of her kingdom, but she did not submit to Azaf Khan. She found there was no hope of success, but her resolve was to die in defence of her country. She marched out with whatever forces she could rally round her standard; she took her son, who was then only fourteen years of age, to fight with her,—she took only those men who were firm in their determination to die by her side defending their dear country.

The battle raged from morning to evening. *Durgabati* saw her dear son fall from his horse severely wounded and carried away by her men. People came to her and asked her to go and see her dying son. "No, I cannot go," replied she, "my men will lose heart, if they don't see me. If he dies, he dies a hero. We shall meet him in heaven." The battle continued for hours and at last an arrow pierced one of her eyes; she tried to snatch it out,—but she failed. Still she did not retire or retreat,—still she fought like a proud lioness and was covered with wounds. Almost the whole of her army had been destroyed; a few only of her faithful retainers were defending her body, so that she might not be taken prisoner by the enemy. She saw that there was no chance of her escape; she would soon be taken prisoner. For once she glanced round the battle-field; for once she looked back to the distant *Gurhmandal* and before any body could know her determination she killed herself by her own sword. It is said that one of her faithful soldiers retreated with her corpse, lest it be polluted by the touch of the Musulmans. It was carried to a distant place and there it was duly cremated. We need not say, that the little kingdom of *Gurhmandal* passed away from the hands of its real masters and was annexed to the Delhi Empire.

THE CHIEFTAIN'S WIFE.

[1]

SULIMAN was the last Pathan king of Bengal. When Akbar established himself on the throne of Delhi, the whole of Northern India submitted to his rule except Bengal. *Munim Khan* was despatched from Delhi with a large army to bring the Pathan Nabob to his senses. Suliman was killed and his son Daud Khan fled to Orissa.

But on hearing the approach of the Moguls, Suliman removed all his wealth to a place, called Jessore, a town in the south of Bengal. This place was the head-quarters of a zaigir, belonging to his financial minister, who was a Bengalee and on whom he bestowed the title of Raja *Vikramâditya.* He was his most trusted servant, and he was virtually the ruler of all southern Bengal, bordering the sea.

In those days Bengal was ruled by feudal system. The native chiefs were fully independent in their own territories and enjoyed all the royal privileges and prerogatives. They were allowed by the Pathan rulers to do what they liked, provided they remitted the tributes to the Nabob's coffer. But often did they rebel and neglect to send the tributes, often did they fight amongst themselves, often did they ignore the existence of the Nabob's power. The chief occupation of the Nabob's army was to force these turbulent chiefs to pay their dues and to prevent them from cutting one another's throat.

When Suliman was killed and Daud fled, Bengal was not conquered. The chiefs stopped payments, —but the Mogul general had little time to look to them. He pursued the flying Nabob from place to place and his hands were full with him. After a year's struggle Daud was killed and his army was broken. His general Katlu Khan made peace with the Emperor and was allowed to rule in Orissa.

But as soon as the Mogul Governor, Raja

Todurmal turned his eyes towards the chiefs, he found they were all in open rebellion. He was driven to take shelter within the fort of Monghyr, where he was besieged by the Bengal chiefs, both Hindus and Pathans. He had to remain in the fort blocked up for a year and half,—but at last with his usual great diplomacy he managed to draw the Hindu chiefs to his side. With their help he soon drove the Pathans away from Bengal and peace was restored. The Hindu chiefs acknowledged Akbar as their Emperor and agreed to pay him tributes as they used to pay to the Pathan Nabob. Raja *Vikramâdītya* followed the example of his brother chiefs, made obeisance to the Mogul Viceroy and went away to his zaigir. He ruled his State peacefully for some years and died at Jessore, leaving a son, named Raja *Pratâpâditya.*

[2]

Pratâpâdītya grew to be a very powerful chieftain. He had a wife, who was known by the name of *Jashareshwari.* It was not known what was her real name,—but she was called after the name of the presiding goddess of the family. It was said that the goddess appeared before the founder of the house and expressed her wish that she would not leave it till there would be an end of virtue and goodness in the family. She also promised to indicate her departure by turning the face of her image, which was in the temple adjoining the palace. Now, there were two *Jashareshwaris* in the palace, one was the goddess, the other was the chieftain's wife;—but perhaps one was in flesh and blood and the other was in stone.

Pratâpâditya grew to be very powerful, at the sametime very vicious. He gathered round him a very large army; all the turbulent characters of the country flocked to his standard. He began to plunder and ravage cities and towns and to exact tributes from the neighbouring chiefs. He united his forces with the Portugese pirates and *Mug* dacoits and set out to ravage the country from one end to the other. It is needless to say that he became too powerful to be punished by the Mogul Viceroy;—he bearded him in his own city and declined to pay tributes or to acknowledge the Emperor as his sovereign.

But he was not satisfied with plundering and murdering the neighbouring chiefs;—he cast his eyes on his own uncle *Basanta Rai.* None was so good as he,—he was a hoary-headed patriarch, loved and respected by all. He did not approve of his nephew's conduct; he tried to pursude him to give up his evil path,—but *Pratâp* put a deaf ear to all his sensible and statesman-like words. He knew he was not loved by his subjects; he knew that his uncle was the idol of their worship,—he was afraid lest they might rise against him and place his uncle on the throne. To make his safety doubly sure he determined to murder the good old man with all his family.

When his good wife failed to induce him to give up the idea of the foul deed, she determined to take a very bold step to prevent her husband from committing such a heinous crime.

There was an old custom, honoured and observed by the chiefs, and which is still in existence in Bengal. When a noble lady required a gallant knight to defend her cause, she would send her *kankan* (an armlet) to a reputed brave man,—or in an assembly of warriors. She would send it by a maid who was asked to throw it down in the middle of the assembly. One of the brave men present would take the gauntlet up and promise on oath to obey the lady's command and to defend her cause till death. Now one day when Raja *Pratâpâditya* was sitting in Durbar,—a maid of the Queen appeared in that great assembly and to the astonishment of all threw the *Kankan* in the middle of the hall. Wonder seized the assembly,

—all anxiously looked to the Chief; but he sat still,—a cloud passed over his stern countenance. At last a warrior slowly rose ;—he was the generalissimo of the army and the brother of the Queen. He advanced towards the *Kankan* and took it up. And then turning towards the chief he said, "This *Kankan* comes from our Queen. I know not what cause to defend; she asks for a knight. As it comes from her,—it was expected that it should be accepted by our brave king, who is her Lord, Protector, Defender and Master. But as he sits still and does not show any inclination to accept the gauntlet,—lest people say there is a lack of brave men in this assembly, I take it up and promise on solemn oath to defend her cause till death."

The king frowned, but said nothing. The maid in her sweet silvery voice pealed forth, "It is the wish and desire of our Queen, it is her command to the brave man who accepts her *Kankan* to defend and protect Raja *Basanta Rai* and his family." "It will be done," said the gallant hero and moved towards his seat.

The king immediately closed the Durbar and retired to his rooms. If he was afraid of any one in this world, he was afraid of his wife. She was in every way worthy to be the wife of

Pratâpâditya ; she was a terrible lioness paired to a savage lion. He called her to him, he caressed her, argued with her, upbraided her ; he tried in various ways to alter her idea of saving *Basanta Rai.* "He is doomed," said he, "he must die, or else we are not safe." "Safe or unsafe" replied she, "I would not allow you to commit such a great crime."

[3]

When *Pratâp* found that it was impossible to kill the old man,—he took recourse to treachery. He appeared to be repentant for his misdeeds. He went to his uncle and fell at his feet; more than a thousand times he asked for his pardon. Raja *Basanta Rai* lived in a castle some miles away from Jessore; he was cordially invited to come to the Raja's palace and he accepted the invitation.

But with all his apparent contrition two persons had grave suspicions of his intention. The brave Rani gave her permission to invite the old Raja, only when she got the Raja's son in her safe custody. The old patriarch before he started for Jessore, took with him one pegion. "If you find" said he to his wife, "this pigeon coming back to you, know then for certain that I am dead or in prison."

The Raja started with a few retainers,—but he was way-laid and murdered by assassins, appointed by the cruel chief. The pigeon escaped and reached the castle in due time. The Raja's wife and family being afraid of further violence and oppression, drowned themselves in the palace tank. The son of the old Raja was saved,—because he was in the safe custody of his aunt, the Rani.

Such a man could not reign safely for long. Raja Man Sing, the greatest of all the generals of the Great Mogul, was sent with a large army to chastise this insolent chief. He arrived at the banks of the Ganges, secured the help of the chiefs and marched towards Jessore. He encamped near the city and sent a messenger to the chief with a *firman*, (a letter of pardon and confirmation), a haulter and a sword. *Pratâp* tore up the *firman* into thousand pieces, took the sword and asked the messenger to take back the haulter. "Tell your general," said he, "to put it round the neck of his master."

So battle was determined upon. *Pratâp* had 52 thousand swordsmen, 30 thousand spearsmen, 10 thousand cavalry, two hundred elephants, and hundred pieces of cannon. Besides all this a contingent from Portugese pirates and Mug dacoits had come to his help. With the major portion of this vast army he went out to give battle. It raged from morning till evening; he had been able to push back the imperial forces and disorganise their entire infantry,—victory was certain to grace his standard, when suddenly a commotion arose in the ranks of his army. They began to break the ranks and fly in all directions. When he asked the cause of all this sudden break-up, he was told "*Jashareshwari* was gone." He could not understand what they meant. "Is my wife dead?" asked he. "No, Maharaja," replied some body, "our great goddess is gone."

We have already told that it was a great tradition believed by all that the great goddess *Jashareshwari* would indicate her departure and with her departure all glory of Jessore would be at an end. A rumour ran like wild fire amongst the soldiers that the goddess had turned her face, which meant that she was gone. They lost heart, they lost all hope of success and fled in all directions. The Raja with all his undaunted courage could not shake off the fatal belief. When he heard what had happened, he was stupified. His embarrasment was taken advantage of by the enemy,—a detachment of cavalry swooped down upon him and in a few minutes he fell a prisoner into the hands of the enemy.

The victory of the imperial troops was complete. Raja Man Sing advanced towards the city,—but he was astonished to see it well defended. On enquiry he found that the brave Rani had assumed the command and had resolved to die in defence of the liberty of her country. Man Sing sent a messenger, demanding the surrender of the castle. "No," replied she, "not till some conditions of surrender are accepted. I know it would be useless bloodshed to defend the castle against the troops of the Emperor. If Raja Man Sing gives me the word of a Rajput that my town will not be looted, and no oppression of any kind will be made upon any of my subjects—I shall surrender the castle without any opposition. There is another condition also,—as a Hindu he must allow a Hindu wife to follow her husband, if that husband is still alive. Tell him all this. If he does not agree, we shall fight, and fight till none will remain alive to endure the oppression."

We need not say Raja Man Sing granted all her prayers. She accompanied her husband to Delhi, sharing with him his prison. But as he was kept in a large iron cage he died on the way near Benares and his wife burnt herself on the same funeral pyre.

THE JODHPUR QUEEN.

DURING the reign of *Shajihan,* Jeswant Sing, Raja of Jodhpur, was the most powerful noble of the Delhi throne. With some thousands of Rajputs he sought to stop the progress of *Aurungieb* when he was advancing towards Delhi to usurp the throne and imprison his father. Near the *Narbada,* a battle was fought; by sunset ten thousands of their number were dead on the field of battle and Jeswant Sing was obliged to retire to his country. It was with a heavy heart he drew near to his capital, for he knew his wife would be terribly distressed and offended on account of the shame and disgrace of his defeat.

The Rani, when she heard her husband was nigh, instead of sending some one to condole with him in his misfortunes, commanded her men to shut up the gates of the castle and not to let the disgraced man enter.

"He is not my husband," cried she, "the Raja of Jodhpur and son-in-law of the great Rana of Mewer cannot be so mean!" A moment after she was of another mood. She commanded a funeral pyre to be made ready, so that she might burn herself. "My husband must be dead," cried she, "he cannot come back alive defeated and disgraced."

In short he remained thus transported eight or nine days without being able to resolve to see her husband. At last she agreed to see him. The gates of the city were thrown open and her husband entered. The Rani, after her anger was over, attended with tender care to her husband's wounds and those of his followers.

Aurungieb, having finally established himself in Delhi, determined to destroy the power of Jeswant Sing, for he was the only man whom he had to fear. Gladly availing himself of a rebellion in Cabul, he appointed the Raja to the chief command of the troops he was sending against it. The Emperor was sure that the turbulent and savage Afgans would capture and slay the powerful Raja and his brave Rajputs.

Jeswant accepted the post, because it was the post of honour and danger. His brave Rani prepared to accompany her husband and share his perils. They left their son Prithi Sing to take charge of the Jodhpur kingdom and with a large force of chosen troops they set out for the campaign against the Afgans.

The brave queen declined to be treated as a woman and a Rani; she adopted the life of a soldier, rode by the side of her husband and went through all the privations of a camp-life. Thus after many days' toil and labour, after hard march over hills and dales, over snow and ice they reached Cabul, and found the whole country in treason. Hardly had they any rest ; they found themselves in uncongenial climate, in snow and ice, amongst savage and barbarian people, beset by all sorts of difficulties and privations. And through all this terrible campaign the Jodhpur queen shared her husband's perils. She followed him as a shadow and fought by his side with the enemy ; her bravery and courage, her power of endurance and fortitude astonished even the strongest and the bravest of the Rajputs.

But alas, Jeswant did not live long. It is every way likely that he met with foul play. His son Prithi Sing was invited to Delhi and received by the Emperor in all honour,—but he soon died of poison. It is said that *Aurungjeb* vowed that Jeswant Sing should never return from Cabul and none of his sons should live to disturb his peace of mind. Some of his assassins must have administered poison,—the effect of which was fatal to the Raja.

The situation of the Rani, away in the wilds of Afganistan without her husband, was very sad indeed. She would have burnt herself with her husband as his loving and faithful wife, but she was prevented from taking the step, for she was expected to give birth to a baby ere many months should elapse. She therefore assumed the command of her faithful Rajputs and defended her post till they could safely retreat towards India.

In a little time the Rani was safely delivered of a boy in the city of Cabul, and when she was able to travel, she with her brave soldiers turned their face towards India. They had to fight their way as far as Peshwar, where they were joined by some more Rajputs, who had started from Jodhpur to bring back their brave queen safely to their capital.

In due course they arrived in Delhi. The Rani and his followers determined to push on for Jodhpur, but they were not to get away without a struggle. *Aurungjeb* demanded that the infant prince should be surrendered to his custody. The Rani flatly declined to obey the Imperial command and her brave Rajputs prepared themselves to defend their infant king and their queen dowager.

The infant prince was placed in a basket of sweetmeats and entrusted to a faithful Musulman, who promised to carry the prince to an appointed place and to keep him in safety till they could appear.

Just after the man had departed with the prince, the Rajputs, buckling on swords and armours sallied forth from the palace they occupied. Their brave Rani was in their midst,—her sword flashed in the light some of them carried. The palace was immediately surrounded by Imperial troops and they endeavoured to cut their way out of the city. Like heroes they fought and like heroes they fell, but a few lived to tell the tale. The battle fought in the streets of Delhi by the brave little band of Rajputs is one of the most glorious acts recorded in the world's history, for it was one against a thousand and it was for their queen, for their infant king and for their fatherland.

When the wounded and bleeding Rani and her few warriors reached the spot,—the hiding place of the infant prince,—they found him safe and sound. With rapture beyond words to express the Rani received her child, and hurrying away with him she rested not till she reached her brother, the great Rana of Mewer. From the Rana she prayed sanctuary for the prince during the dangers of his minority.

She returned to Jodhpur and there nursed the spirit of resistance against the Emperor and supported her son's rights till he was of age to take the field himself against the enemies of their house. The cowardly behaviour of *Aurungjeb* had driven the Rajputs to rise against him,—his attack on a helpless widow and her infanst son united them to take the severest vengeance on the great enemy of the Hindu race. The Jodhpur queen lived to see the shattered state of the Delhi Empire and its final fall. In a good old age full of honours she entered into her rest to join her brave husband.

RANI BHABANI.

[1]

DURING the Mahomedan rule in Bengal, the internal Government of the country was solely in the hands of native Rajas. They were all powerful; they were independent in every respect, except that they had to pay heavy tributes to the central government at Murshidabad, the then Mahomedan capital of Bengal. On many occasions one or the other of these Rajas refused to pay tributes and the Nabob had to send soldiers to make them submit to his authority.

At the latter end of the last century the Mahomedan power began to crumble down. The Emperor of Delhi had become only a name; his vassals and governors had assumed independence and had ignored his existence. But they too had lost their old power and prestige; their authority grew weaker and weaker every day and their tributary Rajas were daily assuming independence and raising the standard of rebellion all over the country.

The last powerful Mahomedan ruler of Bengal was Alivardi,—he was succeeded by a youngman, named Sherajuddaulah. With good deal of difficulty and by shere diplomacy Alivardi made the Bengal Rajas acknowledge his authority, but virtually the disposal of the throne of Bengal was then in the hands of these Rajas. Of these Rajas, four, namely Raja Krisnachandra of Krisnagore, Raja Rajbullava of Dacca, Raja Rai Durlava of Patna, and Rani Bhabani of Natore, were the most powerful. There were two other men who were as influential as they; they were Jagut Set, the banker and Mirzafar, the Commander-in-Chief. These six had the disposal of the throne and they gave it away to the English.

The Natore Raj, over which Rani Bhabani ruled, was as big as Scotland and paid a net revenue of 52 lacs of rupees to the Nabob. The State had an income of a crore and half, besides the expense for the up-keep of an army consisting about 50 thousand foot and horse. Her husband was Raja Ramkant, who succeeded his father when he was only a young man. As often occurs in such cases, the young Raja threw himself head and heart into the whirlpool of luxury and debauchery. His father's dewan, old Doyaram, could not check him; his young wife *Bhabani's* tears and entreaties could not turn him from his evil ways;—he sloped down and down to the awful abyss of ruin and destruction. Doyaram was dismissed and money was spent like water; Government was neglected and soldiers were not paid. Thus one after another many dues to the Nabob were not remitted. Soldiers were soon sent to Natore; Raja Ramkant was deposed and another man was placed on the *Gadi.* He left Natore with his wife and took shelter under the roof of the Jagut Set at Murshidabad.

Debauchery had made him worthless; when he met with difficulties,—when he experienced sorrow and disappointment,—when he had to face wants and privations,—he thoroughly gave himself up into the hands of his most intelligent, faithful and loving wife. Since then he was a nonentity,—what was done, was done by his wife *Rani Bhabani.* She recalled old Doyaram;—she sold all her jewels and bribed all the officials of the Nabob. Some how or other she man-anged to make the Nabob put her husband again on the *Gadi* of the Natore Raj. The husband and the wife left the hospitable house of their friend, or Jagut Set, and came to Natore to the joy of all the people.

But her happiness was soon marred; her husband died leaving her alone and helpless. She had two sons who died in their childhood; she had a daughter, named *Tara,* but she too was a girl-widow. When *Rani Bhabani* lost her husband, she was thirty-two years old. The heavy responsibility of ruling a vast province fell on her when the whole country was passing through a great revolution. But she was up to it; in statesmanship and diplomacy she was matchless. She not only independent of the advice of any dewan or minister, governed her vast State, but commanded her army herself. She was present with her men a few miles off from the field of Plassey to watch the battle in which the British flag was for the first time implanted in the plains of India.

[2]

After assuming the Government she at once saw that she required a very powerful army to protect her State from the ravages of the present Nabob. Readers of the Indian history need not be told what sort of man young Sherajuddaulah was. He wanted money for his debauchery; he had ran through the accumulated wealth of his ancestors,—he wanted more; he required more than what was his just revenue. To get the money he took every sort of means; justice was unknown to him; extortion and persecution became his daily avocations. The native Rajas, who could not withstand his plundering army, were fleeced to death. But to do him justice,—he hardly knew anything of what was done in his name by the unscrupulous scoundrels that surrounded him. He was a mere boy.

Rani Bhabani was intelligent enough to foresee the out-look of the political horizon. She foresaw a revolution in no distant date. She was glad,—for she knew that the Mahomedan power was gone. It was the time for the Hindus;—if they could unite, if they could put aside their petty jealousies and elect a leader,—surely Bengal would become a Hindu kingdom. She was not ambitious; she did never aspire to sit on the throne of Bengal, but she foresaw that there would be a great struggle for it. To be ready to meet it and at the same time to withstand the ravages of the Nabob, she at once began to reform and reorganize her army. Her army soon became the best in Bengal. And it was soon put to a test.

Tara, the widowed daughter of *Rani Bhabani* was a celebrated beauty of the age. Some mischievous rascals about the Nabob plied him with the description of her beauty. They at last got his sanction to get the girl by force if necessary. They wanted to go over to Natore with the Nabob's soldiers and to loot the *Rani's* treasury ;—that was their aim and object and they did it in the name of the Nabob and with the assistance of his army.

They sent a messenger to the *Rani*, demanding her daughter for the lust of the young Nabob. We need not say the messenger of lust was barely kept alive to go back to his principals to inform them that *Rani Bhabani* was not to be dictated. Soon an army was despatched to secure the princess by force, to depose the *Rani* and to loot her treasury. *Rani Bhabani* anticipated it long before the thought entered into the head of the Nabob's satellites. She herself commanded her army, came out of her city and gave them battle. The Moslem army was thoroughly routed and disorganised. They tried to retire to Murshidabad, but *Rani Bhabani* pursued them as far as the outskirt of her dominions.

In fact at that time the whole of Bengal was in arms against the Mahomedans; at every step the Musalman army met with obstructions; their provisions were looted by the villagers and their soldiers were killed wherever they were found.

[3]

In the mean while Sherajuddaulah had made his throne too hot for him; he was beset from all sides; he knew not which side to defend and which to attack. The Rajas resolved to depose him and to place some body else on the throne. Raja Krishnachandra, Raja Rajballav and Raja Rai Durlav met in the house of Jagut Set; they invited *Rani Bhabani* to join in their deliberation. Jagat Set proposed Mir Zafar for the throne, saying that he had promised to follow their advice and to rule Bengal as benignly as possible. He was the commander-in-chief of the Nabob,—the Musalman army was under his command, so placing him on the throne could be managed without the shedding of blood. "Maharajas and friends," said *Rani Bhabani*, "could it not be managed to place a Hindu on the throne of Bengal? This is the time and opportunity." "*Rani*," replied Raja Krisnachandra," who is there that does not wish it? But for thousands of years we are under foreign yoke; we have no prestige and no sufficient forces to defend the country from foreign powers; besides we are badly in want of unity and we are full of jealousy. To place a Hindu Raja on the throne would mean civil war; and taking advantage of it perhaps the *Marhattas* would snatch from our hands the throne. They are a people thoroughly unknown to us, and cruel to the extreme. We are living with the Musalmans for years, we know them and they know us,—so it is better to have one of them than any one else."

"I admit," said the *Rani* "the weight of your argument, but suppose after getting the throne Mir Zafar becomes as bad as Sherajuddaulah, what would be our remedy?"

"We have thought over it," said Raja Rajbullav, "and therefore to keep Mir Zafar under check, we have thought of asking the help of the English. They are a very powerful people,—they are mere traders and they never think of getting a kingdom. If we give them some trade advantages, they will always be at our disposal. With their help we shall always be able to keep Mir Zafar under check."

"Besides," said Jagut Set, "Sherajuddaulah has already destroyed their fort at Calcutta. Surely they would try to punish him. If the new

Nabob, whoever he be, do not make friends with the English, he will have to fight with them at the very begining of his reign."

"I have heard," said Raja Rai Durlav, "they have defeated the Musalman Nabob of the Deccan."

"Maharajas," said *Rani Bhabani*, "I am but a woman and dare not advise you in such high political matters. But suppose they become as cruel and ambitious as the Marhattas! Suppose they after the taste of the sweet of Government forget their trade and aspire to be the rulers and kings! What would then be our remedy,—what will be then our means to check them?—They are more foreign than the Marhattas; we know nothing of them. I am not for Mir Zafar, I am not for the Marhattas, I am not for the English. We are in many ways bound to the family of Sheraj,—depose him by all means, but put some scion of the family on the throne."

Thus the discussion was continued for hours, till *Rani Bhabani* was induced to give her consent to place Mir Zafar on the throne with the co-operation of the English. The *Rani* gave her consent with reluctance, but when she gave her consent she said, "Maharajas, I am bound to abide by your decision, but my mind says this revolution would not be good for the country; the English would be supreme in the end. So instead of placing some imbecile Mahomedan on the throne,—when we cannot unite to place one of us on it and when we cannot trust the Marhattas, let us hand over the throne to the English. They might be good people; let us take our chance."

"Let us try Mir Zafar," said Raja Krisnachandra, "if he fails,—we shall then call the English in."

So every thing was arranged. Readers of history know all about the Battle of Plassey. Sheraj fled and Mir Zafar joined the English. *Rani Bhabani* watched the battle from a distance and then she marched away with her army to Natore.

Clive came to Murshidabad and took possession of the Nabob's treasury. He placed Mir Zafar on the throne in all formalities, secured every sort of privilege for the English and retired to Calcutta.

[4)

For some years a great revolution passed over Bengal. The throne of Bengal was put to the highest bidder by the English and it was sold and resold and sold again. Mir Zafar was deposed and

Mir Kashim was placed on the throne. Within a very short time Mir Kashim was driven out and Mir Zafar was again made Nabob ; and so on, one after the other. But these revolutions lay confined within the precincts of the palace at Murshidabad. All over Bengal there was peace and contentment,—for neither the Nabob nor the English had time, opportunity or mind to interfere in the internal Government of the country. In fact at the time of which we are speaking Northern Bengal was governed by *Rani Bhabani*, Southern Bengal by Raja Krisnachandra, Eastern Bengal by Raja Rajbullav and Western Bengal by Raja Raidurlav. They were friends of both the Nabob and the English; they regularly paid in their tributes and there was no complaint against them. So long they lived, Bengal was very happy,—peace and contentment reigned all over the country.

Thus the latter portion of the life of *Rani Bhabani* was passed in peace and contentment. She had appointed able dewans to administer her State ;—she had made rules and regulations and every thing passed on smoothly till her death.

As she had nothing more to do—to organize or improve her State, she adopted a son and vested him with all the powers. She then determined to pass her time on the banks of the holy Ganges in prayers and meditations.

A few miles higher up from Murshidabad on the opposite bank of the holy river, *Rani Bhabani* built a palace round which a town gradually grew up. Here did she pass the remainder of her glorious life, flooding the country with her charity. A vast amount was every year given away for the encouragement of the Sanskrit learning; innumerable poor and helpless men and women were fed and pensioned. Temples with charity houses were built all over the country; countless tanks were dug to do away with the scarcity of water. In Benares she built many temples and established many charity-houses. It is said that she used to spend at least 25 lacs of rupees every year in charity.

In the year 1803 she died at the ripe age of seventy-nine, just 46 years after the battle of Plassey. It was fortunate for her that she died or else it would have been her misfortune to see the political changes with their concomitant oppressions, extortions, persecutions, tyranny and injustice that soon after took place in Bengal and in which the English were the chief actors.

She left her adopted son Raja Ramkrisna to govern her vast State,—but he adopted the life of an ascetic. He gave away in charity almost whole of his possessions, the rest was sold for the mismanagement of the State. Only a little of the great Natore Raj remained in possession of the family, when Ramkrisna died, and that little still belongs to the scion of *Rani Bhabani's* family, who lives at Natore, a station in the Northern Bengal State Railway. The holder of this ancient State is honoured by the British Government with the title of Maharaja Bahadur.

THE BANKER'S DAUGHTER.

[1]

WE shall narrate the career of another high-born girl, who flourished during the reign of Sheraj. The Nabob was a young man of twenty, he was brought up in luxury and indulgence, and was spoiled by his grand father, Alivardi, the late Nabob, on account of excessive caresses that were showered upon him and misled by companions who were the scums of the society and who were the greatest scoundrels that ever walked the streets of Murshidabad. He and his companions began to commit all sorts of horrible crimes; young wives were snatched away from the sides of their husbands,—daughters were ravaged before the eyes of their fathers, and sisters before their brothers. No woman's honour was safe during the short reign of the great debauchee.

He did not spare even his most powerful nobles; he openly demanded their beautiful daughters and sisters,—and where open demands were not preferable, he adopted secret means to decoy and dishonor the girls.

Now, the Jagut Sets were the richest men in Murshidabad. They were the Rothchilds of India. Their banking houses lay scattered all over the country. There was not a small town in India where one of their branch houses did not exist. Powerful Rulers and Potentates were their debtors, —even the great Emperor had often to come to their doors to borrow money. Thus they were the richest and the most honoured men in India.

Matab Chand Jagut Set was the head of the house, when young Sheraj ascended the throne of Bengal. He had a most beautiful daughter, named *Ashamanya* (matchless),—perhaps none was so beautiful in Murshidabad as the Banker's daughter. Wicked Sheraj grew mad to possess her. But she was no other than the daughter of the most influential man in all India! The Nabob dared not openly demand her.

One night he dressed himself as a woman and entered the palace of the rich banker. He passed unchallenged to the quarter where the beautiful *Ashamanya* lived. Perhaps he had no other intention but to see her and admire her beauty, but when he stood before her and gazed at her sublime beauty,—a beauty the like of which he never saw,—he forgot where he was and tried to embrace her. She was alarmed ; she fled from the spot, she ran to her husband and told him what had happened. The outraged man ran after the disguised Nabob, caught hold of him when he was escaping from the house and gave him a right royal shoe-beating. The Nabob barely escaped with his life, but never forgot the insult and the disappointment.

A few days after, the poor husband was openly murdered in the public street. The heartless Nabob ordered the man's head to be severed from his body. He placed the head on a silver plate and sent it as a present to the proud daughter of the banker. We need not describe her feelings of horror and indignation. The unhappy girl when she heard what had happened went into hysterics and in a few days symptoms of insanity appeared in her.

[2]

Such and many other acts of violence to the

powerful nobles and chiefs of the kingdom soon ensured the ruin of Sheraj. The throne of Bengal was always at the disposal of its powerful chiefs from the time when their old king went away to pilgrimage, leaving it to be occupied by the Pathan General. These chiefs now resolved to remove the wicked and vicious man and to place on the throne *Mir Zafar* the Commander-in-Chief. They invited the English merchants to come and help them in removing the cruel tyrant. In the field of Plassey, *Mir Zafar* stood aloof with his soldiers. One company of the Nabob's force attempted to fight with the English, but they soon received the command to stop from the Nabob, who passed the fatal order on the advice of *Mir Zafar*. The English General, Clive caught the situation at a glance; he ordered his men to rush forward. They made a bayonett charge with a shout and soon the Nabob's great army was at a rout.

He fled towards Murshidabad; finding no safety there he fled again towards the west, but he was seized at Bhagabangolla and brought down to the city. By the order of Miran, the son of *Mir Zafar*, one Mahomedi Beg beheaded him. His mangled corpse was thrown on an elephant and carried through the streets of Murshidabad to be buried like that of a felon. *Ashamanya* was in a stupor all this while. Since the day of his husband's murder till the day of Sheraj's death,—she remained a raving maniac ; sometime as an idiot,—sometime as deaf and dumb, but often she became a very violent woman. Her father placed her under the treatment of best physicians,—but to no effect. On hearing the murder of Sheraj, some one suggested to take her to the place of burial. "If she sees the blood and the mangled corpse of her husband's murderer," said he, "her vengeance might be gratified and she might recover her senses." The suggestion was acted upon. She was taken to a place from which she could see the last end of him who murdered her husband.

After two years and a half she appeared to be a little rational. She looked at the corpse fixedly for some time and then turning to one of her maids she asked who was the poor man whose body had been thus mangled and what crime he had committed. "My lady," replied the maid, "He is your husband's murderer. He is the tyrant Nabob, who has at last been justly dealt with." She appeared not to understand the purport of her maid's reply. Then suddenly flashed a flood of light into her brains. "Oh, Oh!" cried she, "take me back home, take me back home!"

They carried her back to the palace; she appeared to be very calm; she talked with her mother and others quiet rationally. They were all astonished and pleased to see that the insanity had at last left her. But she now and then said, "God has done what I should have done. When he has done my duty and work, I shall do what he should have done. I shall do *His* work and *His* duty." None could understand what she meant, and when they understood her meaning, it was too late; *Ashamanya* was gone.

[3]

She had gone where no body knew. At the dead of night she slipped out of the house and fled, where she herself did not know. The blood of her husband's murderer and his horribly mangled corpse had filled her with a new idea. Her brains reeled with the thought which said, "*Ashamanya* should have taken the severest vengeance on the murderer of her husband. She should have dethroned him, killed him, mangled him,—but God has done all that for her. Ever merciful and ever loving God should have protected him, should have done him good,—should have loved him, bad as he was. When He has not done it,—

He must have surely left it to be done by her. Yes, she must do it." She resolved to do some good to Sheraj,—but alas, his mangled corpse was rotting underneath the earth across the river! He must have left some object of love,—there must be at least some one, whom to benefit would benefit the dead man. The thought made her mad,—she left the house and fled.

She came to Bhagabangola and heard a story which filled her heart with joy. She was told that only one,—out of thousands that accompanied Sheraj when he left his great palace at Murshidabad, went to share his perils and to be a partner of his woe as she was a partner of his weal. Her name was *Meherunesha* Begum,—but Sheraj called her "*Gul*" (Rose.) She was his wife,—ever neglected and ever hated by her husband, who was always sunk in debauchery and carnality. But in his misery she was the only one found amongst his innumerable friends and relatives to be true to him. She was only 16 years old;—she was advanced in family-way, but she followed her husband and ran by his side over the thorny grounds and jungle roads.

At Bhagabangola she gave birth to a pretty daughter and Sheraj was obliged to stop for a few days to allow her time to be fit for the journey. For him it was a fatal halt! We have already said he was found out and killed. Poor Girl! The once Her Highness the Begum of the mighty Nabob Nazim of Bengal, Behar and Orissa, was left uncared for in the house of a poor woman who took compassion and gave her shelter. She lived in her house for a month and half, when she heard that a woman was enquiring after her. She was not afraid of her safety; all her love and attention had now centred in her baby. She must be saved from the ruffians who had murdered her husband! She must go to Delhi and plead the cause of her baby before the mighty Mogul! Therefore when she heard that some body was enquiring after her, she was terrified and hiding her baby within her clothes she fled.

The half mad banker's daughter followed her from place to place, but she never got the opportunity of meeting her. Poor *Gul* knew that some body was shadowing her; how could she know the intention of her pursuer! She fled from place to place like a hunted hind till she was almost caught on the banks of the Ganges by her persevering pursuer. It was just after three years from the day of the murder of her husband,—for these three years she ran from place to place to escape from the woman who was following her like a blood-hound,tracing her steps from town to town, from village to village,—just after three years, she at last almost fell into the hands of her pursuer. It was an awfully stormy day,—a great cyclone was raging over the country ; trees were uprooted and houses were pulled down. When men and beasts were trying to protect themselves from the fury of the storm, poor *Gul*, with her baby on her breast, ran towards the surging and roaring Ganges. Mad *Ashamanya* was not far off ; she was running after her and shouting to her,—but her voice did not reach the frightened girl in the roar of the storm.

[4]

She came and entreated the boatmen to take her on the other side of the river. She had a very valuable ring on her finger, the last of her wordly possessions. She offered it to the boatmen who could ferry her across. At last one man's temptation for money rose over his sense of safety. He agreed and *Gul* jumped on the boat. When *Ashamanya* came to the bank, she saw the boat dancing on the stormy and foaming waves of the roaring river.

As the mad woman stood staring on the fury of the water, the boat suddenly disappeared There was a loud shreak and *Ashamanya* leaped into the tempestuous river below. She struggled with the mad waves,—on and on she swam, the waves dashed on her as if they would reduce her to atoms,—but nothing like a firm determination! She came where the boat had disappeared a few minutes before. She saw a bunch of black hair floating above the waves—she caught them and dragged insensible *Gul* towards her. She saw her child was still in her breast tightly grasped by her loving arms. She tried to snatch the child from her, but without avail. As she was a very strong swimmer she kept them all afloat and allowed the waves to carry them where they liked.

After three hours she touched ground; she dragged *Gul* to land and tried to carry her to a hut near by. The fury of the storm had much abated,—but alas, the poor girl was dead! With good deal of difficulty she revived the child, but poor thing,—she had lost her power of speech!

We have very little more to say. *Ashamanya* lived with this child somewhere in East Bengal, where in many households she and her adopted daughter are still worshipped as godesses.

THE BANDIT LADY.

[1]

WARREN Hastings was the first Governor-General of the British possessions in India. The Nabob of Bengal had been pensioned of,—the military and finance had been taken charge of by the English and the old feudal government had been thoroughly destroyed by the new comers. The new rulers considered the chiefs as mere collectors of revenue,—as ex-officio servants of the State and their possessions were no better than lands leased out to them for certain annual rent. Many of the chiefs were taken aback by the novel system of Government introduced by the English ; many declined to submit and many broke out in open rebellion. But they were no match for British cannon, they were everywhere defeated and driven out of their castles; many of their territories were confiscated, many were hanged and many rotted in prison. Only those, that could bribe the Calcutta officials, escaped from confiscation, torture, imprisonment and death.

Thus the whole country passed through a great revolution; anarchy reigned every where. The outlawed chiefs turned high-way robbers and decoits. They ravaged the country, looted villages and towns and did what they liked with their weak neighbours. There was none to protect the weak; the Nabob was gone,—the English did not care to look to the country. Their only aim was to get rich within the shortest possible time and to go back to their distant home. Ever happy and peaceful Bengal passed through a great crisis.

Now, the whole of Western Bengal from the borders of the districts of Beerbhoom to the banks of the Ganges fell prey to a very powerful band of robbers, who defied the Nabob and laughed at the English. They were in full possession of this vast tract of country,—looted rich people at their pleasure, and plundered cities and towns in day-light.

Wonder of wonders; the leader of these robbers was a lady! None knew what was her name, but some called her *Rani Ma*, some *Gouri Ma* and some again *Devi Choudhurani.* Hardly any one out of her chosen band ever saw her,—none knew where she lived and who she was. None knew whether she had a husband or she was a widow,—none knew the reason why she turned to be a bandit. But her name was a terror not only in Beerbhoom, Burdwan and other adjacent districts,—but all over Bengal. Women hushed their children by calling the name of *Gouri Ma,* and peaceful chiefs shuddered when they heard of *Devi Choudhurani.*

As we have said the Nabob had not the power to quell the disturbance and disband these robbers; the English had little time to think any thing else but how to get rich. Thus *Devi Choudhurani* and her band were left to do what they wanted. Soon it was apparent that she had changed her aim. She was no longer a bandit-lady, but had assumed the regal garb and had declared herself the Queen of Bengal. She had gathered round her not only robbers and thieves,—but she had formed a very powerful army and many of the chiefs had joined her standard. She did no longer keep her intention secret; it was openly declared that her aim was to drive both the

the English and the Moslem from Bengal and to make her country independent and free.

Although all this was known all over Bengal,—people outside her rank did never see her and never knew where she lived and which castle she had made her head-quarters. But it was evident that she was no longer a Bandit Lady,—but an acknowledged Queen of Bengal, whom its chiefs served and paid tributes.

[2]

When the news of this band of robbers first reached Calcutta, the English officials laughed to hear of it,—for what they cared for a band of thieves, the leader of which was a Bengalee woman ! When their outrages and plunderings were reported to Mr. Hastings, he replied he had more important matters to look to than to hunt after a Bandit Lady.

Thus unchecked *Devi Choudhurani* grew daily more powerful and prepared for the great struggle. So long her men confined their *loot* within a certain limit,—but now orders were passed to loot English treasuries and to drive the English out of the places where they lived. One district treasury after another fell into their hands,—one official after another came to Calcutta to tell the tale of revolt, massacre and *loot*. One day at dead of night they came stealthily to the very heart of the Metropolis and looted the house of a very rich native banker in Calcutta. The English soldiers came out, but before they could come to the rescue, *Devi Choudhurani* and her men had disappeared.

The Governor General was at last convinced that the Bandit lady was not a thing less important than the *looting* of the treasury of Chait Sing or the hanging Raja Nundkumar. The English were terrified, for they distinctly saw rebellion all over the country; they felt the people had at last risen to throw off the shackles under which they had been labouring from generation to generation. They believed that this *Devi Choudhurani* was a myth,—she had been held up by the designing men to excite the people, telling them that their great goddess had appeared to help them in their attempt for gaining freedom and liberty. They urged the Governor General to get ready immediately an expedition against the robbers and to suppress the rebellion without further delay.

An expedition was soon despatched. We need not describe their doings; suffice it to say that the Bandit Lady and her men were defeated at every step. They were pushed back from place to place, dispersed from cities and towns, and hunted down in jungles and strongholds. At last the English met with a strong resistance. The robbers fought like demons: every inch of the ground had to be won at the point of bayonet. They fought like heroes and fell like heroes,—the English also suffered a great loss. At last they were able to drive the robbers back to a castle, under the walls of which they took shelter.

As the English advanced they met with a heavy cannonade. Arrows and bullets were showered upon them from the ramparts;—a band of the robbers suddenly issued forth from a jungle and attacked their flank. The battle raged for three hours and the English strewed the ground. One gun from the gate of the castle was scattering death amongst their rank. The English commander resolved to stop it; he called for volunteers and rushed with them to pike the gun. There was a desperate fight near the gun,—the robbers stood to their gun till each and every one of them were bayonetted. But one was still alive and still managing it with wonderful skill. One Rajput Sepoy rushed towards this hero and raised his long *Talwar* to cut him down. He jumped upon the gun and warded the sword of his assailant;—but he was soon overpowered,—an English soldier leaped upon the gun and bayonetted him.

It was found afterwards that the hero who so bravely fought at the gate of the castle was a woman. Some identified her body as that of the *Devi Choudhnrani*. But many said, she was not killed, but disappeared into the sky when her men were killed. Be it what it may, her name is still revered and respected all over Bengal.

AHALYA BAI.

[1]

ONE of the most important Marhatta sovreignties is the kingdom of Indore,ruled by the Holkar Dynasty. In the year 1765 Malahar Rao, the Ruler of Indore, died and was succeeded by his grandson Mali Rao. Now, this prince was the son of Khandi Rao and *Rani Ahalyabai*, the former of whom was killed by the Bhils,—the latter lived a vary retired life as a strict Hindu widow. But Mali Rao lived a very short life and died without any issue. There was none to succeed him to the throne of Indore. Thus his mother *Rani Ahalya Bai* was obliged to give up her retired life and to take up the Government in her own hands. She was a woman of extraordinary intellect, courage and tact. More than one hundred and fifty years have passed and still the name of *Rani Ahalya Bai* is honoured all over the southern India. Many kings and queens came and went after the death of *Rani Ahalya,*—but none was so loved, adored and admired as the queen of Khandi Rao.

As is the case all over the world with wicked men, when they find an oppertunity to satisfy their avarice or ambition, they forget what means they adopt to do it;—so was the case in the kingdom of Indore. When they found a weak woman, as they took *Rani Ahalya* to be, on the throne of Indore they wanted to deprive her of all her power, to take away the management of her government from her hands and to fill up their pockets by looting her treasury and robbing her people. But, alas, they found *Ahalya* a very hard nut to crack. She was not a weak woman; she was neither an idiot, nor a timid girl; she was an able sovereign—abler than all the rulers that ever sat on the throne of Indore. She managed the government thoroughly in an independent way; she did not allow any one about her to interfere in State matters; she appointed only capable men in higher offices of the State; she kept a very sharp eye on every department of her Government, without allowing any body to take any indulgence or to neglect his duties or to any way oppress her people. Thus she weeded out all wicked men from her court and cleared her Government off all that was bad and vicious. It is needless to say that many took offence,—the wicked and the vicious burnt with vengeance; and soon there was a conspiracy to depose her. One Gangadhar Jashabant took the leading part; he was the priest of the royal court, and consequently expected to have good deal of influence over the court and Government. But *Ahalya Bai* did not allow him to interfere in any state matter. "Reverend father," said she, "I shall always obey you in religious matters, as I am bound to do;—but I shall most humbly pray to you not to interfere in matters which do not concern you."

Her words enraged the priest; he induced Raghubdada, the uncle of Madhu Rao, one of the rulers of Indore, to join him. He was a man of great influence and power, respected and feared by all the people. Some other influential chiefs and officials also joined the consipircy; many of the disappointed candidates for high posts hastened to fan it, and soon it took a gigantic shape.

The conspirators threw up their privacy and openly sent a latter to *Rani Ahalya*, asking her to adopt a child and appoint a regency, for as the letter went on, "You being a woman are not a fit person to remain on the throne of Indore, when it is threatened by the Rajputs on one side and the English on the other."

[2]

Rani Ahalya was too sharp for the conspirators. She kept a very careful watch on the movements of every one of them, since Gangadhar Jashabant hatched the conspiracy. She was thoroughly prepared for it, and had already made all arrangements to ward it off. The conspirators were dogged and watched ; spies were set upon them, soldiers were secretly kept near their houses and places of meetings. The army was ordered to be always in readiness for emergency, and she herself was ready to take the field any moment.

When her arrangements were all complete, she replied to Raghubdada and the conspirators. "Do not think I shall allow you to threaten me or to do anything to raise the standard of rebellion in my kingdom. I am a Marhatta woman, so you must be careful how you displease your Queen and sovereign. As I apprehend mischief from you, I have ordered my officials to arrest you and to throw you into prison." No sooner did the conspirators receive her letter than they were all arrested and sent to prison, before any of them could make any attempt to oppose her.

Gangadhar Jashabant apologised to the queen and was allowed to appear in the court. Other conspirators were released on their taking solemn oath of allegiance. Raghubdada was set free and asked to leave the kingdom of Indore. But he did not forget the indignity which he brought down upon him by his hastily joining the conspiracy. He could not however pardon *Rani Ahalya* and watched an opportunity to wreack his vengeance on the best of women of his race. He secretly communicated with the Rajputs and induced them to invade the kingdom of Indore.

But *Ahalya* was watchful; she was never taken by surprise. She knew what Raghubdada was doing and she expected that sooner or later the Rajputs would invade her country. She had been making preparations for it; she appointed one Tukaji Holkar,—a man, though very low-born, was qualified in every respect,—the Commander-in-Chief of her forces. Perhaps none was such a great General as Tukaji Holkar and under him *Rani Ahalyas'* army became most formidable.

The Rajput chiefs, with the hope of receiving secret help from Raghubdada and knowing that the Government was in the hands of a woman, boldly crossed the borders of the Indore kingdom. They took possession of Nimbhaira and drove away Shibnānā, the Governor of the fort. As soon as the news reached Indore, the queen at once despatched two of his Generals, Tukaji Sindhia and Sribhai, with five thousand soldiers to hasten to Shibnānā's help. She herself followed them with her most powerful army. But she had not to plunge herself into a bloody compaign. Tukaji Sindhia and Sribhai retook Nimbhaira and drove the Rajputs out of the town. They retreated back, hearing that *Ahalya Bai* was herself coming with a very powerful army to give them battle. They left Indore kingdom and so long *Rani Ahalya* was alive, they never ventured again to cross the borders of the kingdom of Indore.

[3]

Rani Ahalya was not only a heroic woman always ready to lead an army,—but she had great proficiency in statecraft and diplomacy. So long she was on the throne of Indore, there was peace and prosperity all over the kingdom. When she assumed the Government, the whole country was infested with robbers, Thugs and Decoits; there was no peace any where; life and property were very unsafe. *Rani Ahalya* declared, in open court, that whoever would be able to clear his kingdom off the] robbers, she would give him her daughter in marriage. One Jashabanta Rao, a young noble, took upon himself this important task and he was successful in his undertaking. So long *Rani Ahalya* was alive, there was not a single case of decoity in any part of her vast kingdom. As promised she married her daughter princess *Mukta* to Jashabanta Rao, the hero, who exterpated all robberies and decoities from the kingdom of Indore.

She was very strict in the administration of justice; she appointed able men as judges and herself heard all final appeals. She never allowed her officials to oppress any of her subjects. Once on a time at a village called Basia, one rich trader named Sirkam Dass died leaving a widow in possession of a vast amount of wealth. The bereaved wife proposed to adopt a child, but the collector of revenue put obstacles in her way.

He did all this in his zeal to increase the State revenue; for if the widow did not adopt a child, the wealth of the trader would all finally go to the State treasury,—but as soon as *Rani Ahalya* came to know the facts, she at once sent for the collector, reprimanded him and allowed the widow to adopt the child.

On another occasion, two of her rich subjects, Talpadas and Baremdas of Kargram, died childless. Their widows came to the queen and prayed to her to accept the immense wealth left to them by their husbands, as they wished to retire to holy pilgrimage. "Sisters," replied the *Rani*, "I thank you for your kindness, but I am rich enough to require or wish for more. Go, spend the sum in digging tanks where there is scarcity of water,—in building charity-houses where there is want for them and in such works as may benefit the public." The *Rani's* suggestion was accepted and the money was spent on charitable and useful works.

She used to live a very simple life; she never indulged in luxury or pomp. Even in State occasions her dress was simple as possible. She was an embodiment of economy; and all the money thus saved she spent in useful public works and necessary charitable institutions. There was hardly a village in her kingdom where she did not dig a well or a tank; there was hardly a village where she did not establish a charity-house. Her innumerable temples are still to be seen all over the country,—especialy her celebrated temple of *Bisnupada* at Gya, which is one of the best architectural productions of the Hindus. She left a large amount of money for the future support of the temple. The temple of *Bisnupada* is one of the most important pilgrimages of the Hindus; even the poorest of the Hindus goes once in his life to the *Bisnupada* to do homage to his dead parents and they all carry the name and fame of *Rani Ahalya* to the remotest part of the country.

She did not forget even the birds and beasts. She kept reserved in every village all over her kingdom a plot of land as pasture ground for birds and beasts; there were many *pinjarapoles* or hospitals for old and decrepit beasts in many towns; it would take many pages more to enumerate all the good works that she did in her thirty years' peaceful reign.

In the year 1795 *Rani Ahalya* died to the greatest grief of all the people of Indore;—why Indore?—her good works extended all over India and her name was adored from the Himalayas to the Cape Comorin. India wept for her death, for there would be many a long year before she would be able to count another *Ahalya* amongst her glorious daughters.

PRINCESS KRISNA.

[1]

BEAUTIFUL *Krisna Coomari* was the daughter of the Maharana of Udaypur. She was known as the "flower of Rajastan." None was so beautiful and accomplished as Princess *Krisna* of Mewar. Chiefs and potentates from far and wide cast longing eyes towards her and many a messenger came from many states with the offer of marriage. But the Rana chose for her Raja Jugut Sing of Jeypur. The Chief of Jeypur, as soon as he learnt that his offer had been accepted, sent a detachment of three thousand troops with a formal proposal and preliminary presents.

A bloody war raged over this proposal of marriage. The whole of Rajastan turned into a great battle-field,—blood flowed like water and internal dissensions rented the country. Innocent *Krisna* was the cause of this struggle. Her beauty became the cause of the ruin of Rajputana. The great Rajput race destroyed themselves by a suicidal war.

Raja Mani Sing of Marwar, who was one of those who were anxious to secure the hands of the beautiful Princess, advanced pretensions for her on the ground that she had been betrothed to his predecessor. He sent an ambassador to the court of Mewar and wrote to the Raja that as the Princess had been betrothed to his predecessor so she was betrothed to him also. He was now the ruler of Jodhpur, therefore the Princess was his rightful claim and the Rana was bound to give her in marriage to him. He gave distinct hint that if his proposal was not accepted he would not hesitate to take arms and force the Rana to do his bidding.

The Rana of Mewar was not the great and powerful Rana as his fore-fathers were. He was still respected as the head of the Rajput race but his influence was nominal. His vassals had become more powerful and commanded larger armies than he could boast of. Besides the Rajput power had been broken down. Their continual fight with the Mahomedans had crippled them,—the flowers of their chivalry were laid in ashes. The Marhattas under the Scindia were ravaging their country, looting their cities and enforcing black-mail from all the chiefs. Even the Maharana had to pay heavy *chouts* to buy peace. The brave Rajputs, that were able to struggle with the Mahomedan hordes and to keep their heads up when all India bowed down at the feet of the great Mogul, were now like sheep in the hands of the Marhattas, who murdered and butchered them at their pleasure. This was not all. A Mahomedan had become all powerful in the very heart of the holy land of Rajasthan. He had become the Nboab of Tonk; his name was Amir Khan. He was one of the most notorious villains India ever produced. He played upon the broken down Rajput chiefs; he now took the part of one and then throwing him overboard took the part of another.

Such was the state of Rajputana when a great struggle broke out amongst the chiefs for the hand of the pretty Princess *Krisna.* Powerful Scindia took the part of the Raja of Marwar; Nabob Amir Khan pretended to be the greatest friend of the Rana. The most of the Rajput chiefs took the side of Raja Juggut Sing of Jeypur.

Scindia advanced with a force of eight thousand men and encamped near the city. He demanded that the Rana should dismiss the embassy of the Raja of Jeypur and refuse to give his daughter to him. He must marry his daughter to the Raja Mani Sing of Marwar. Poor Rana was too weak to withstand the Marhatta attack. There was no alternative, but to dismiss the nuptial party and to agree to whatever was demanded. The Jeypur chief prepared to avenge this great insult and gathered together such an army as had not been seen in Rajputana even in the days of its glory. The Raja of Marwar hastened with his army to re-inforce his friend, the Scindia. A terrible struggle took place; there was great slaughter on both sides. But neither party confessed to be beaten and neither party relinquished his claim to the fair object of the war.

[2]

In the midst of this great struggle an unhallowed suggestion was made known to the Maharana. The blood-thirsty Khan of Tonk suggested that the torch of discord should be extinguished by the blood of the innocent cause of the quarrel. With indignation and rage the Rana listened to the proposal that the life of his most beloved daughter should be the price of reconciliation between the two hostile candidates for her hand. Great pressure was put upon him by the wily Amir Khan and he at last gave his unwilling consent. The fatal order was passed that *Krisna* should die.

But it should not be the work of a common executioner. Who was to do it? Who was so hard-hearted in all Rajputana who could thurst a poniard into the lovely breast of the Princess! Raja Dowlat Sing, a relative of the Moharána, was first called upon to carry the order into execution. He was horror-struck. "Accursed be the tongue that commands it!" Exclaimed he, "Am I to keep my allegiance to the Maharana at such a price? Dust on my allegiance, if thus to be preserved!" He refused to obey the order and left the palace in great indignation.

Raja Jowan Das, a half brother of the Princess, was then called. The dire necessity of the deed was explained to him and he was asked to perform it. "Father," said the Prince, "Is it really your command that I shall kill my dear sister?" "My son," said the Rana, "They say it is a necessity for the sake of our country." He accepted the poniard and went to the apartment of the Princess.

Krisna stood before him in all her youthful loveliness,—innocence, grace, sublimity played on her countenance. She welcomed her brother in her usual warmth and asked what command he had to give her. "Sister," said the Prince gravely, "prepare for death." *Krisna* smiled and then she laughed out. "I am not joking," said the Raja, "It is the command of the Maharana. You must die for your country. Sister, it is for the great struggle that was de-populating the happy land of Rajas han." Princess *Krisna* became grave, she looked at her brother and then looked back to her beloved maids. "Brother," she at last said, "Many princesses of our house died for our country and you will not find your sister unworthy of that great house. It is the command of our father that I must die,—I am ready. Take me to the place where I can do it. What is more glorious for the daughter of a Shisodia than to die for her country!" "Well," faultered the prince, "I am commanded to—to—." "Brother," said the Princess, "I understand. Come and do your duty, and with it help your poor sister to do hers." Sobs were heard amongst the maids who stood behind their beloved mistress. *Krisna* turned towards them and said, "Dear friends, don't weep for me. Be glad and know that I die very very happy. If my blood can stop the carnage of Rajasthan,—let it flow,—oh, let it flow. Thousands and thousands of homes have been made miserable."

The Prince could stand no longer. His brave heart quelled before the glorious calmness of the Princess. He flung the poniard through the window and fled from the room. One after another, the order was given to many;—for the first time in the annals of Mewar the Princes and the nobles flatly refused to obey the command of their Maharana.

The news of the sacrifice spread like wild fire through the palace and the shrieks of the frantic mother were heard, as she implored mercy for her child and called down heaven's vengeance on the world. *Krisna*, alone, of all the inmates of the royal house, appeared calm and resigned to her fate.

But none was found to execute the foul deed. All anxiously looked to the Rana for a retrieve; every one expected that he would withdraw his cruel order. But, alas, he was helpless! He had fallen into the cruel grasp of Amir Khan. He would not listen to a refusal. The Princess must be killed or he would kill all the members of the royal household. The whole of Mewar would be ravaged and the Rajput race would be annihilated. Amir Khan was in a great hurry to finish the job; for he was told that innumerable Rajput chiefs from every part of Rajasthan were hastening towards Udeypur to save the Princess from her cruel murderers and to prevent a great national scandal. Amir Khan knew all this and forced the Rana to hasten the cruel murder.

No one being found to take the life of the maiden with a dagger,—poison was ordered to be administered to her. The deed was left for women to accomplish, the hand of man refused it. One of her maids brought the cup and presented it to her in her father's name. Loud lamentations had filled the palace.—none had heart to speak and all were weeping; sobs were heard from all quarters and the raving imprecations of the queen-mother pealed through the house. But the lovely victim shed not a tear; when the cup was offered to her, she bowed her head and accepted the fatal liquid. She then bade adieu to her beloved maids, asked the blessings of her mother, prayed for her father's long life and silently took the poison.

She pleasantly conversed with all till the nauseating draught refused to assimilate with her blood.

Again the bitter potion was prepared. She drank it, but it was rejected again. As if to try the extreme of human fortitude, for the third time the fatal liquid was administered and for the third time Nature refused to aid the horrid purpose. But the blood-hounds were impatient till their victim was at rest. They made another and a fatal attempt. A powerful piate was presented. She received it with a smile and drank it. The desires of barbarity were at last accomplished. She slept!—a sleep from which she never awoke. The wretched mother did not survive long. In a few days her body was carried to the funeral pyre.

MAHARANI JHINDAN.

THE name of Maharaja Dulip Sing is known to all Englishmen and his sad history is also known to all readers of Indian history! A few years ago he was a prominent figure in England and his towering stature with his oriental Pagri was one of the chief features of all Court functions. His beautiful country-seat was the favourite recreation-ground of the Prince and the Princess of Wales, the other royal princes and princesses and almost all the prominent peers of the realm. He was taken into the English aristocracy and parties of the peers and peeresses were never held without him.

Maharani Jhindan was the mother of Maharaja Dulip and the youngest and the dearest wife of the Lion of the Punjab, Maharaja Runjit Sing. Her real name was *Chandrabati*, but she was popularly known as the Maharani Jhindan. We need not say she was worthy of being the wife of Runjit Sing,—a man who consolidated the Sikh nation, made it a great power amongst nations and extended his sovereignty from Cabool to Delhi; a man who was respected and feared even by the English, who had at this time virtually succeeded to the sovereignty of Delhi and a man who created a new force in the Khalsas, with whom the British soldiers had to fight the greatest battle in India. When Maharaja Runjit Sing died he left three sons behind him, namely Kharga Sing, Sher Sing and Dulip Sing; but he left behind him innumerable ambitious and designing officers and generals, who were merely kept under check by his super-human talent, but who just after his death fought like wolves to enjoy the sweets of power and to usurp the throne of the Punjab. Kharga Sing was soon murdered and was succeeded by his brother Sher Sing, but he too met the fate of his brother. Within four years two of the sons of Maharaja Runjit Sing were murdered and removed from the throne. The whole country was rent with civil war, disorder and anarchy; one minister after another and one general after another attempted to usurp the power, but was murdered and removed. Finally Prince Dulip Sing, who was then only five years of age, was declared as the Maharaja of the Punjab and his mother, Maharani Jhindan, took the reins of Government in her own hands.

She was a woman of great intellect, unconquera-able courage and stupendous energy. She was the fittest queen for the unruly and brave Sikh nation. She was as powerful in council as in war; in fact she had in her character almost all the traits of that of her great husband. She consolidated her power,—amicably settled the quarrels and rivalry of the ministers and generals,—brought peace and contentment all over the country and made the Khalsa army as powerful and invincible as it was under her husband. She appointed the most capable men to the high State situations; the bravest and the cleverest generals were given charge of regiments; and she appointed Sher Sing, the greatest of all the generals, the Commander-in-Chief of her army.

The frontier of the English possessions was analogous to her kingdom. The English were alarmed by her able management of the Punjab Goverment and by her wonderful reorganization of the Sikh army. They thought it their interest to place soldiers all along the frontier of their possessions and congregate a large army on the banks of the river *Satadru.* The Sikh complained that the English had encroached upon their territory and the English replied that the Sikh had entered the British possessions. Whatever be the cause, the great Sikh war broke out and continued for a year.

In this great war Maharani Jhindan was virtually both the Queen and the General. Many of her faithless and ungrateful officials and generals secretely began to help the English. There was a time when she stood almost alone to defend and to protect the liberty of her country and the great name of her illustrious husband. But she wavered not,—she stood as firm as a rock, guiding her armies and managing her kingdom without the help of any of her ministers and generals. The great Sikh war is a matter of history: there were great battles fought at Mudki, Ferojepur, Allewala, Sobraon and other places,—battles, the likes of which the English never fought in India. What could Maharni Jhindan do in the face of the treachery of her own officials and generals? Her army had to meet defeats after defeats, till she was obliged to sign a treaty. When one of her generals came and informed her that her army had been defeated in the battle of Sobraon, she heard the news in her usual calm dignity and then said, "My Khalsa must fight again." When one of her great ministers advised her to stop the war she said, "I am doing what my husband would have done. So long I am alive, I would not see my Punjub taken possession of by the Ferengee." So the war continued till at last she was obliged to ask for peace.

A treaty was signed by which the English posted John Lawrence as their Resident at Lahore and the queen was made to consult with the Resident in all State matters. Virtually the Government came into the hands of the British Resident, who tried by private means to remove the Maharani to make the British power paramount in the Punjab. But it could not be done openly; so the help of statecraft and diplomacy was taken. In the name of the young king Dulip, who was then only twelve years of age, they charged Maharani Jhindan with acting against the interest of the king and the sovereignty of the Punjab. They made the young king sign a decree of banishment against his own dear mother. Maharani Jhindan was removed, first to Shekpur, and then to Benares.

When the official came to her with the decree of banishment and informed her that she would have to leave the Punjab, she simply said, "Who has passed this decree?" The man told her that it was the work of the young Maharaja himself. Well," said she, "I must obey the king. I am not the sovereign of the Punjab,—I am only his mother. So I must go; you need not be afraid of me. I would not oppose or incite rebellion against my own son. I know, all is lost."

She was first removed to Shekpur, but afterwards it was thought proper to send her to the holy pilgrimage of Benares. This was done only to please the Khalsa army, to which she was a goddess of adoration. When she was informed of this, she said, "All the same. What does it signify if the prison house be in a holy or an unholy place!" She came to Benares and lived very quietly,—but the shock was too much for her. She wept not for her son, not for her present imprisonment, not for the loss of power and riches, but for the Punjab, but for liberty and the glory that was lost for ever. Her heart broke drown; she fell seriously ill and lay in the holy city at the point of death.

The news of her illnesss reached the Khalsa army and the people of the land of five rivers. To them she was a goddess,—a heroine,—a lady for whom they could sacrifice their lives. The great British diplomacy and the unpatriotic conduct of the Sikh officials and generals did not prevent the Khalsas to rise against the English.

The second Sikh war is also a matter of history. The British army under the command of Lord Gough was hopelessly defeated and for the time being the Sikh power was in ascendance. But at the battle of Guzrut the Sikhs were defeated, their army was broken up and scattered to five winds. The British Government thought it proper to remove Dulip Sing to England and annex the Punjab. He was converted to Christianity and was allowed a handsome pension. He subsequently married an English lady and had some children born of her.

Maharani Jhindan lay ill at the holy shrine of Benares, uncared and unlooked of. For years her misery was extreme; she had delirium of the severest kind, in which she cried out, "My brave Khalsa,—on to the battle,—the spirit of your old master is over you. Defend and protect the liberty and the glory of the Sikh nation."

At last the British Government was moved to pity; her condition was most heart-rending. What could give her solace in her dying days! Was there nothing that could pacify the dying moments of the once great Maharani of the great Sikh nation! The British Government thought if she could be placed by the side of her son, she might be at peace; at least she might die happy. They brought her down to Calcutta,—but then the once great Queen of the Sikhs had become a delirious woman. She was placed on board a steamer and sent to England to join her son. But death soon relieved her of all her miseries. She died on her way to England and was buried at sea.

THE RANI OF JHANSI.

[1]

JHANSI was a small State in Central India. *Gangadhar Rao* was a Marhatta chief, who ruled over the dominion and acknowledged the authority of the British Government. He died in the year 1853 leaving behind him his wife, *Rani Lakshmi Bai* and an adopted child, bequeathing the kingdom to this boy and authorizing his wife to administer the State in his minority. The English Goverment had bound themselves to act according to the last wishes of the Marhatta Chief, but the Governor General, Lord Dalhousie, changed his mind and annexed the little kingdom of Jhansi. The poor widowed Rani removed herself with her child to a town away from Jhansi and there she passed her time brooding over the great wrong done to her by the English and formulating means to avenge it if possible.

Lord Dalhousi's annexation policy raised alarm throughout the length and breadth of India. Discontent and half-suppressed rebellion raged all over the country. People began secretly to form themselves into bands, and whenever a person of influence showed the least sign of forming a secret conspiracy, hundreds of people rushed to his standard. *Lakshmi Bai* of Jhansi was dead against the English; she was a brave woman; she was intelligent and heroic. She had long determined to make an effort to regain her kingdom by force. Her people were all on her side,—her old ministers and generals had promised to help her, if she could up-raise the standard of revolt; there was no want of men who were willing to enlist themselves as soldiers to fight against the English. *Rani Lakshmi Bai* secretely and slowly raised up the nucleus of a very powerful contingent, which became soon after invincible to arms.

Fortune favoured her. Just three years after her husband's death, in the beginning of 1857 the great mutiny suddenly broke out all over India. The native Sepoys stationed at Mirut mutineed and massacred their European officers,—the native troops of the Maharaja of Gawalior refused to obey their officers and openly declared that they would join the Sepoys and fight the English. Maharaja Scindia of Gawalior stood by the English and moved towards Agra, but major portion of his soldiers went towards Cawnpur to join the Marhatta chief, Nana Sahib, who had assumed the leadership of the Mutiny.

Lashmi Bai found this as the best opportunity to wreak her vengeance on the English. She armed herself and marched out with her soldiers and rode at their head towards Mirut to join the mutinous Sepoys and the Gawalior contingent.

We need not say she was heartily welcomed. She was the wronged and persecuted Rani of Jhansi; she hailed from one of the highest and most respected Marhatta royal families;—her name was known to all and sympathy of all the people was on her side. Therefore when the mutinous Sepoys found her to join them, their courage and enthusiasm increased a hundred-fold and with loud acclamations they welcomed her to their rank. As for Gawalior contingent, they had lost their chief and leader. Their Maharaja had left them to their fate and had thought fit to side with the English;—they were as a flock without a shepherd. When they saw the Rani of Jhansi marching towards them with her sturdy Marhattas, they were filled with courage and enthusiasm and at once thought it fit to follow her standard. And again, she was but a woman , but she had armed herself,—she had placed herself at the head of her army to fight with the English to recover the freedem of her country. Who was there in that large assemblage of soldiers and warriors, whose heart did not beat quicker and whose blood did not run faster in order to march at once to the English camp to fight for the liberty of his country or to die in the noble attempt.

[2]

The whole of the memorable Mutiny has been disfigured by most unprecedented cruelty and shedding of innocent blood. There could be no jutification for the massacre of the English women and children. Never in the annals of India warriors were found to be so cowardly as to raise their swords upon helpless women and children. But the Mutiny was the work of low class ruffians who were picked up by the English Sergeants and enlisted as Sepoys. They had no sympathy from the members of the noble houses, and they kept themselves aloof from the Mutiny, or else India would have been lost to the English.

We have searched through every page of the history of the Indian Mutiny, written both by friends and foes of the Indian people and we have not found any of them charging the Rani of Jhansi with the massacre of women and children. She never allowed her soldiers to participate in these bloody cruelties; she often tried to dissuade the Sepoys from the path of cowardice and ruffianism,—and when she failed to turn them from cruelty and murder she separated herself from them and went away with her men to some other place.

After the massacre of Cawnpur the British troops re-took it and General Windham was left in charge of the city, the Commander-in-Chief Sir Collin Campbell, marching to relieve Lucknow. Windham was defeated by the Gawalior Contingent, —one wing of which was commanded in person by the brave and heroic Rani of Jhansi. But Sir Collin soon came back;—there was a great battle fought on the back of the Ganges.—93 Highlanders under their brave Commanader Hon'ble Adrian Hope charging the mutineers and breaking their ranks and the Blue Jackets under young Peel sending shell after shell after the flying Column.

Lashmi Bai from the begining of the outbreak of the Mutiny till the final overthrow of the Gawalior Contingent remained with the mutineers, fighting side by side with them in many of the celebrated encounters with the English; but she had no sympathy with the conduct of the Sepoys; with reluctance she stuck to them as long as it was possible for her to do. But she finally retired with her men to Gawalior, broken-hearted and almost with all hopes of success lost.

General Sir Hugh Rose was sent to pursue her and disperse her band. In one of the most well-organized retreats the Rani of Jhansi made for Gawalior; at times she turned back upon her pursuers and gave them battle; in more than one battle she defeated General Sir Hugh Rose who was daily reinforced, whereas her limited number of followers became fewer and fewer. She had no mind to fight, but to take shelter under the walls of the forts of Gawalior or Jhansi, but the English General forced her to fight again. Just at the outskirts of the town of Kalpi *Lashmi Bai* turned upon the English General like an enraged lioness and gave him battle,—her little army was annihilated but she escaped with her life and fled towards Gawalior. There the soldiers welcomed her in open arms and there she again tried to make a last effort to regain the freedom that was lost.

Readers of history know that when the English made a breach in the wall of Gawalior fort and when the bold Highlanders were rushing towards the breach bayonetting the Marhattas, *Lashmi Bai*, the Rani of Jhansi, rushed out with her faithful retainers and cut her passage through the English.

She fled towards the south and was soon joined by the Marhatta leader Thantia Topi. She then tried to rally round her scattered army, but was soon baffled by the English General. The brave Rani had no rest since the beginning of the Mutiny; she was always on her steed, looking after her army and encouraging her soldiers with her noble presence.

The English army soon came to her peel. There was a great batte, but fortune was againts her. Tanti Topi left the field in hot haste and her men lost heart. They began to fall back,—some of them began to fly. She tried to rally them, but her men could not stand the charge of the English cavalry. Upraising herself on her steed she again and again called her men to stand firm,—but alas, the day was lost! The English Horse fell upon them like thunder-bolts and scattered her little army to four winds. She would not still leave the field,—a few of her faithful men were still by her side and they were earnestly entreating her to save herself by a flight, but she would not turn her horse's head. Finding her inexorable one of her men took hold of her horse's bridle and dragged her on and on from the field. But the British cavalry with their lances up came rushing upon them. Her horse stumbled and before she could manage to raise him up, a lancer cut her down.

Her brave Marhattas turned and hastened to defend her, but alas, they were too late! But they rushed on under a heavy cannonade and rescued her body from the unholy touch of the enemy.

Quietly they placed it on the funeral pyre and under the shade of night marched away to the south.

A GROUP FROM THE MUTINY.

[1]

DURING the sad days of the Indian Mutiny,—there were not only women like the Rani of Jhansi who fought and died for her country, but there were many more who suffered and heroically stood the persecutions and tortures of the infuriated Sepoys to protect helpless English women and children. An Ayah was in the service of Colonel ——who was then residing at the head quarter station of Oudh. She was in charge of the child of her master and mistress, the child being only a year and half old. On the day on which the Sepoys suddenly broke out into open mutiny, she, as, usual went out with the child for an airing. On her way back she heard the mad uproar of the mutinous Sepoys;—she hid the child under her clothes and hastened home. But she found that her master and mistress were gone,—all the Europeans had left the town to save their lives and the Sepoys were looting the Banglows and murdering the Europeans without sparing even women and children. She did not know what to do; she was at the point of leaving the house with the child when she heard the noise of the rebels near at hand. She immediately hid the child under some clothes and sat near it. She resolved to save it or die in the attempt. The Sepoys were soon in the room, "Where is the Ferengee brat?" they roared. She said she did not know, her master and mistress must have taken her away. No, they have seen the child with the woman; they must have it or her head would be severed. She again and again protested that she knew nothing of the child when a Sepoy lost all patience and gave her some severe cuts. She fainted and the rebels left her to loot other houses.

When she recovered she looked for the child. Her joy knew no bounds when she found it safe and sound. Under the cover of darkness she crawled with the child to her home and there painted it, in order to change its color, so that none might know it to be a European baby. A few days after she came to learn that her master and mistress were in Lucknow. With much difficulty she reached the place, saw her master and placed the child in the arms of her mistress. Should we attempt to describe their joy and their gratitude towards the poor woman? But they could not help her,—for they were beset by the rebels from all sides. They promised to show their gratitude in some tangible shape when peace would be restored. As her wounds were not healed, she left Lucknow and came back to her home.

After the suppression of the Mutiny, she went to Lucknow and searched for her master and mistress. Alas! they were both killed and the child whom she saved from death by risking her own life had been sent to England with other orphan boys and girls.

[2]

Another Aya,———was in charge of the child of Mr.——stationed in Cawnpore. When the place was besieged by the rebels under the leader Nana Sahib, the English found it impossible to defend the city. They asked for a safe conduct to Allahabad and agreed to surrender the place if they were allowed to go away in peace. Nana agreed and the English came out and marched with their women and children towards the river. When they got into the boats, the Sepoys suddenly began to fire upon them. The Aya, finding no escape, jumped down from the boat with the child and her son who was about 15 years old. She hid the child within her bosom, took her son by the hand and ran towards the bank. But alas, there stood hundreds of rebel Sepoys with open swords. As soon as they saw a white child with the Aya, they rushed upon her and attacked her from all sides, " Give us the boy," said they, " and you are safe." " Not till I am alive, " replied the woman, " save us both if you expect grace from great God." "Mother, mother," cried her son, " give the Feringee boy or else they would kill us all ." " Let them kill me," said she, " I won't give them the child till I am alive." A sword flashed,—the head of the poor woman rolled down the beach and the chid was tossed up. When it came down, the monsters received it on the points of their sharp bayonets and laughed aloud. The son of the heroic Aya escaped with his life and lived to narrate the glorious deed of her mother.

We shall speak of another Aya, named *[illegible]*, who

was in the service of Dr.——,the Cantonment Surgeon of Oudh when the Sepoys of the place broke out into mutiny. As soon as the news reached the Doctor he immedietely sent away his wife and three children to Lucknow in charge of a faithful servant. Mrs. ——could get no time to take any of her valuables,—she could not take even her jewels. She fled with her children in a country cart, hidden under some sacks of fodder. *Bamni* was not present when her mistress left the place, but soon she came and found that she had left behind all her valuable jewels. She bundled them up in a piece of flannel and took them to her home. A few minutes after the Sepoys looted the house and set fire to it. *Bamni* saw the destruction of her master's house, but was glad that she had been able to save the best portion of it. She dug a small pit behind her hut and kept the jewels hidden there without the knowledge of even her own relatives. When peace was restored she searched for her master and learnt that he was in ————. She left her home with the jewels and safely delivered them to her mistress.

[3]

Though one *Rani* fought with the English and

joined the rebel Sepoys,—yet another *Rani* helped them in their greatest need. Raja of Bundi, a powerful and heroic chieftain of Rajasthan, joined the rebel colour; he collected all his men and marched out to meet Nana at Cawnpur. The English with all their women and children fled from their cantonments; many were butchered on their way to Delhi, but some escaped into the jungle. They had to meet the greatest privation,—they had no food for days together; their shoes were torn and their clothes were tattered to rags. Mothers carried the children on their shoulders and plodded through the thorny jungles under the burning sun of Rajputana;—many succumbed on the way and some had to be carried on the backs of their companions.

The dreadful news of this privation and misery reached the *Rani* of *Bundi* whose husband had gone away to massacre the English. If she liked, she could have followed the example of her husband and killed those helpless men and women; but no,—she had a larger heart than that her husband ever possessed. Risking her own life she determined to succour the helpless. She despatched some of her trusted servants to the place where the English had halted out of sheer exhaustion. She sent words to them to be at ease, for she promised them safety so long they would be in her country. She said she would also try to give them a safe passage to Delhi. She supplied them with food, clothes and shoes; she procured for them some carts. She enjoined some of her faithful retainers to accompany them till they would reach Delhi in safety. The English knew not how to express their thanks to this greatest of great heroines,—a heroine who dared to succour the enemy of her husband in their greatest need. They determined to see that justice was done to her by the British Government on the restoration of peace, but alas, she did not live to see it!

Her husband, soon after, returned to his capital, being pushed to the wall by the brave English General Sir Hugh Rose. He heard what his *Rani* had done; he was mortally offended and he ordered her to be siezed and thrown into a dungeon. But he had no breathing time,—the English cannon boomed at the gate of his castle and hundreds of rifles rattled around his city. The Raja collected a few of his men that still stood by him and went out to give them battle. He fell fighting and his city was filled with British soldiers. Sir Hugh Rose at once enquired of the *Rani* and sent her words that she and her Principality were safe, for the kind acts done to English men and women in distress. But alas, he was informed that the *Rani* had been beheaded by the order of the chief a few minutes before he went out to battle! The English flag flew half mast on the tower of the conquered castle in memory of the brave *Rani* of *Bundi*.

[4]

When mutiny broke out at Fayzabad Mr.—, Deputy Commissoner, had time only to intimate one of his faithful servants to take his wife to the riverside where boats had been procured to remove the ladies and children. Mrs.——fled hidden in a palankeen, but soon it was found that the rebel Sepoys were coming in that direction. A village woman saw the *Meer Sahib*; she also saw the Sepoys at a distance; she came running to the palankeen and asked the lady to follow her, or else she should be surely killed. Mrs.——, finding no other means of escape, jumped out and ran after the woman. She kept her hidden in her room in an earthen hut and stood at the doorto mislead the rebels. But they had seen the lady, they came to her and enquired where the white woman was gone. "I don't know," she firmly replied. "You don't know!" cried the rebels, "you rascally bitch."

And they began to beat her. She stood all their persecutions and did not give out where the lady was. The rebels went away and Mrs.——passed the night in her hut.

Next day she reached the boats in safety with the help of her saviour, and started with some other English ladies and children towards Delhi. This village woman was not the only person that succoured them in their need by risking their own lives. They dared not come to the bank for the fear of the Sepoys and soon their provision felt short. Children cried for milk and no milk was to be had. They at last were forced to venture to the coast to save the children from starvation. Some women were taking water; but the village was full of rebels, thus venturing out to procure milk meant total destruction. But the women, when they found the children were dying for milk, came on the boats and fed them from their own breasts.

APPENDIX.

MIRA BAI.

[1]

IF you travel over the vast country, extending from the banks of the Ganges in the east and to those of the Indus in the west, from the Himalayas in the north to the Vindyas in the south, you will notice a particular name mentioned in the most popular songs sung in the Hindi language. The cow-herd boys in their noon-day songs, the religious devotees in their devotional psalms, the celebrated songsters in their musical *soirees*, the dancing girls in their public entertainments ;—all sing the name of *Mira ;* in every song you will hear the name of *Mira Bai* mentioned.

Who is she ? If you ask any of the people whom

you will meet,—either he or she, be a boy or a girl; an old man or a woman,—he will at once bow his head in respect and will reply, " Oh, Sir, she was a great lady." *Mira* is known to all,—young and old, men and women;—nay she is not only known, she is loved, admired, adored and worshipped as one of the angels of the Hindu race.

She was the greatest devotee amongst women, —she was one of the greatest poets of India. She was the queen of the mightiest Principality in the land of heroic Rajasthan, but she assumed the garb of an ascetic, left her husband's royal palace and sang the name of her loving God in the sweetest strains that were ever heard in India.

She was born in *Nerata,* a mere hamlet in the hilly Rajputana, but she descended from one of the most respected families in all Rajasthan. And perhaps none was so handsome as she. In the heroic land of the Rajputs, she was considered the Lily of all Lilies.

The best flower of Rajputana always graced the palace of the Maharana of Chitor, who was the head and acknowledged paramount Lord of all the Rajput clans. *Mira* was married to *Kumbha Sing*, the heir-apparent of Chitor and on the death of the old Rana, she became the queen of Mewer.

Both she and her husband were poets from

their very birth. The major portion of the prince's and the princess' time passed in composing and reciting poetry. But gradually the line of the composition of the husband and the wife differed. The prince grovelled in worldly matters, the princess soured high into celestial regions.

She read much of *Srikrisna*,—she felt the presence of the loving God in the person of the beautiful cow-herd boy of *Brindabana*. She felt that none can be happy in this world or can expect to be happy in the world next without loving the Fountain of Love, the great God of the Universe. She saw God in flesh and blood in *Srikrishna*,—she felt that she was one of the maids of *Gukula*,—she felt that she was gone,—gone to the happy land of celestial love. All her compositions turned on God and on God in flesh,—the loving boy of *Brindabana*. All her songs were directed towards him and all her poems told men that love to God is the only means for salvation.

[2 [

Time wore on; she became the queen. She became more independent than before and her loving husband and king allowed her all scope to gratify her wishes.

Religious fervour,—the great love that was bred in her,—the great devotion that inspired her,—carried her gradually far, far away from the world. She neglected her toilets, her household duties, her worldly affairs. Day after day, and night after night she passed with her maids in singing the name of God. Her composition was exquisite, her voice was matchless, her singing was super-excellent. With all her natural qualifications—with her beautiful composition, voice and mode of singing,—her songs breathed the great love,—the charming pathos,—the deep feelings with which her heart was full. Her maids were carried away with her sweet songs,—they sang and danced with her and forgot the existence of the visible world.

But how long *Mira* could remain imprisoned within the walls of the Chitor fort? One, in whom the great love had appeared, could not remain confined in a palace. She felt uneasy,—she went to the temple in which was the image of *Srikrisna.* There sang she, there danced she till she lost herself in elysium. She fainted; her maid hastened and caught hold of her. They placed her on their laps and tried to bring her to her senses. She recovered and returned home.

From that day daily went she to the temple

and there sang she in her sweet way the name of her loving God. Whoever heard her songs was melted to love God and to love her;—from tens to hundreds, from hundreds to thousands, men flocked from all quarters to hear her songs,—to join her in her great *matinee*,—to follow her in the path of happiness and glory. She almost left her palace and lived in the temple of the God who was the idol of her heart. Hundreds lived with her and thousands carried her name and fame to the remotest parts of India.

[3]

Her fame reached the Great Mogul. World-renowned Akbar was the great Emperor of Delhi. He was a man who knew how to appreciate men. His court was the seat of all the great men of arts, science and learning.

When he heard of *Mira Bai*, he was eager to hear her songs. Though Chitor did not bow its head to his throne, yet the Maharana was not in deadly enmity with him. But *Mira* was a Hindu lady, she was the *Maharni* of Chitor; he knew Chitor and its Rajputs once fought to the last, because a Moslem Emperor wanted to see its queen. He knew that the queen with all the women of the city burnt herself to save the dishonour of being seen or touched by the *Musalmans*. He knew the pride of the Hindu race and their great sanctity for their women. He dared not openly propose to see *Mira* and to hear her songs, lest he might set up a great war in Rajputana. He called his musician *Tan Sen* and consulted with him on the matter. At last it was settled that the Emperor and the musician in the disguise of Hindus would go to the temple af Chitor, where the *Maharani* daily used to come.

They came alone and unattended. They saw her; they heard her songs;—the Emperor was so carried away that he fell at her feet and entreated her to teach her the means of attaining salvation. But he soon got rid of the mad infatuation and religious fervour that possessed him on account of her charming songs and their unspeakable pathos. He rose and took out a jewelled necklace from his clothes. He presented it to her and said, "Most respected lady, kindly accept this humble present and put it round the neck of the God of the temple."

Mira took the chain and then looked at the disguised Emperor. "Beloved Sir," said she, "this necklace seems to be very valuable. May I ask where from men like you, who appear to be ascetics, can get such things?"

" Madam," replied Akbar, " I picked it up from the Jamuna when bathing and therefore thought that I could not do better than present it to your God."

Mira thanked them for their love of God, and the Emperer and his muscian went back to Delhi.

But the diamond necklace brought misery in her most happy life; it destroyed her domestic happiness, it cost her the love of her dear husband. The necklace was so valuable that its presentation was soon noised abroad. The king desired to see it; it was appraised by crown jewellers and they valued it at ten lakhs of rupees. One of them identified it with one which was sold to Akbar, the Emperor of Delhi. Enquiry was set on foot, and the identity of the two strangers was tried to be found. How long the disguise of the Emperor could be kept hidden! The king was informed that the Great Mogul himself came to see his wife; he has touched her and presented her with the necklace. Well, she had lost her honour,—she had become an outcaste; she had brought dishonour and disgrace on the great house of Mewer! Order was at once passsed that she should die.

[4]

But none was found to execute the royal order.

One after another all the officers of the State refused to obey the royal mandate. A death-warrant was drawn and signed by the *Maharana* asking the queen to kill herself. When she was returning from the temple after her daily *Puja*, one of the ministers of the State placed the document in her hand. She glanced over its contents and asked the bearer of the death-message whether she could see her husband once. "Your Majesty," said the officer, "will see in the paper that the Maharaja destinctly says that he will not see Your Highness." "Well," replied *Mira*, "tell him that his wife will obey his command." She was accompanied by many men and women; she knew they would be heartily grieved to hear the royal order and therefore she did not mention anything to them, but silently passed into the palace.

At dead of night she rose and changed her royal dress. She wore only a piece of ordinary cloth and left the palace. None knew that she was gone; all were asleep and all were in deep rest. She left behind her all that was dear and near to her; she went away throwing the whole city,—nay the whole country, into the greatest grief.

She came on the bank of a river; she stood there for a few moments and then jumped into its wavy breast. She knew not what happened; her brains reeled; she saw a supernatural light dancing before her eyes and then she lost her consciousness. But she felt she did not die; she saw a vision. A creature of brilliant light appeared before her; the angel bent down and kissed her; she smiled upon her and said, "*Mira*, you have obeyed your husband and you have killed yourself. But you have a higher task to perform, a higher duty to do. You are to teach people the great love that makes mankind happy. Go and do it."

When *Mira* opened her eyes she found it was day. The sun was shining frightfully in the sky and the whole country was burning in its scorching rays. She had been washed on the bank; just by her side the river was running forwards in its course. She raised herself up, she looked around her, but she found no living thing as far as her eyes could see. She rose and she went on singing the song of God.

She walked on and on till she met a few cowherd boys. "My beloved sons," said she, "can you direct me to *Brindaban?* Can you tell me the way by which I can reach the great pilgrimage?"

The boys gave her milk; they called her mother and went with her to show her the way to *Brinda-*

ban. She walked on and on singing the name of *Hari*, and her sweet songs filled, with celestial sweetness, all the villages through which she passed. Men and women started from their works and came to see who was passing; boys and girls ran from their plays and followed her crying "*Hari, Hari*."

She walked on and on; many satisfied themselves by offering her presents which she declined to accept; many again came to her with choicest eatables, which too (except milk) she returned with thanks. But some left their home and hearth and notwithstanding her repeated requests followed her footsteps. From one, her followers and admirers rose to be thousands; when she entered the holy land of *Brindaban* it appeared as if the great goddess of *Kailash* had come with all her followers of ghosts and spirits;—so mad were the men who followed her in religious fervour.

The news of her appearance in *Brindaban* spread all over the country. Her sweet songs, from mouth to mouth, had reached the remotest parts of the country. *Mira's* songs were sung in village homes and royal palaces. Those that saw her and admired her in Chitor hastened to meet her in *Brindaban* and those that never saw her became so eager to see her and hear her that thousands flocked towards the holy city. The mighty *Maharani* of Mewar was no longer a queen but a beggar woman, full of the great love that gives mankind salvation and that makes this world a heaven on earth.

[5]

There was a great saint in *Brindaban*, named *Rup Gosain.* He was a man of great devotion and asceticism,—he was a man of vast learning and deep thought, but he never used to see the face of a woman, for his motto was, "Never see woman and coin, if you want salvation."

Mira heard of his name and sent him a message. "Tell him," said she to her messenger, "that *Mira* knows that there is only one man in *Brindaban* and that man is *Srikrisna.* All others, that live here, live in his love and therefore they are all maids of *Gokula.* If *Rup Gosain*, being a male has stealthily entered the ladies' appartment of the palace of our lord *Krisna*,—it is high time for him to fly, lest he be found out by any of the maids and chastised by the king."

The saint was much pleased with her message.

He at once knew *Mira* was not an ordinary woman. He invited her to the temple where he lived.

Mira came, fell at his feet and asked his blessings. "What," said *Rup Gosain*, "can I do for you, my daughter?" "Father," said she, "allow me to live in this temple, so that I might learn from your lips the words of God." Thenceforth she lived in the temple; people said *Rup Gosain* had become her desciple,—but *Mira* said she was a desciple of the great saint.

Time went on in singing and dancing. Thousands of men and women came to join with her in singing the name of *Hari*. Her songs of God and his love filled the atmosphere of *Brindaban* with the sweetness of heaven. They were echoed and re-echoed throughout the land, and men and women on the Himalyas, on the banks of the Jamuna and the Ganges, in the land of the five rivers, in the distant country of the Marhattas,—nay, even on the coasts of the deep blue ocean, sang the songs that were sung by *Mira* on the steps of the temples at *Brindaban*.

Need we say Chitor was no exception? In every street, in every lane, in every house, high or low, were heard the songs that ended with the words "*Mira says so and so.*" Wherever the

Rana turned, he heard the name of his wife mentioned. He saw his wife had risen to a higher kingdom,—a kingdom to which his sovereignty was nothing. He at last felt that *Mira* had not disgraced the great royal house of Mewer,—she had bestowed upon it the greatest possible honour. Well, she had banished her, she had ordered her death, for the fear lest people would cry shameupon his family for the unholy touch of the Emperor. Now, he did every thing to please the people,but the people were not pleased ; they had followed *Mira*, All the world were loving his wife,—he must be a scoundrel not to go to her, ask her pardon and bring her back to her royal palace.

He left his palace in disguise and walked all the way to *Brindaban.* He found *Mira* sitting alone on the steps of a temple and singing the name of *Hari.* He accosted her and begged for alms. "Well," said she, "I am a beggar woman. You should go to some rich man."

"But," replied the disguised king, "a honest beggar comes to a beggar for help."

"Tell me," said *Mira*, "what can I do for you?"

"Pardon me," exclaimed the king and removed the guise, *Mira* stared at her husband and then fell at his feet. "Dear husband,—my lord,"—cried she, "have you at last remembered me?"

We shall not attempt to describe the happy meeting! The husband and wife returned to their happy home and *Mira* lived half of the year in *Brindaban* and half in Chitor.

She was not for stern asceticism She asked men to live in their homes, doing their ordinary duties,—but always in love and devotion towards their God. We shall translate one of her songs to show her opinion on this point.

"If to remain in water gives man salvation, then all acquatic animals must get it."

"If vegetable diet gives it, then monkeys and other beasts and birds surely would get it."

"If eating grass gives it, then deer and goats would get it."

"If to leave one's wife means salvation,—then every eunuch would get it."

"*Mira* says, nothing but love of God can give man salvation."

We have nothing more to say; in fact we know very little of the great woman who has left behind her marks which will never be destroyed so long as the Hindi language and the Hindu race exists. Pity it is that India had never historians! What little we know of *Mira*, we know from annals and tales. But her sweet songs will exist till the final destruction of Hindusthan. Her spirit will breathe over every Hindu home till the final collapse of the Hindu race.*

* We have purposely placed *Mira Bai* in an appendix. The reason of it is that the characters and careers, of those that have been placed in the body of the book, are quite different from that of *Mira*. They made names in worldly matters, but *Mira* is known by her divine love. She was but one amongst many that have immortalized the holy land of Ind,—but she was perhaps the best amongst the best of them.